Simple Home Baking

Simple Home Baking

Over 90 irresistible recipes for cakes, muffins and other sweet delights

Carol Pastor

NH
NEW
HOLLAND

To my mother, Eileen Everest, who has coloured my life with her wonderful bakes.

CY CP

First published in 2005 by
NEW HOLLAND PUBLISHERS (UK) LTD
London • Cape Town • Sydney • Auckland

Garfield House
86–88 Edgware Road
London W2 2EA
www.newhollandpublishers.com

80 McKenzie Street
Cape Town 8001
South Africa

Level 1, Unit 4
14 Aquatic Drive
Frenchs Forest, NSW 2086
Australia

218 Lake Road
Northcote
Auckland
New Zealand

10 9 8 7 6 5 4 3 2 1

Copyright © 2005 text, illustrations and photographs
New Holland Publishers (UK) Ltd

ISBN 1 84537 046 5

Senior Editor: Corinne Masciocchi
Design: Isobel Gillan
Photography: Ed Allwright
Food styling: Pippa Cuthbert
Editorial Direction: Rosemary Wilkinson
Production: Hazel Kirkman

Reproduction by Colourscan, Singapore
Printed and bound by Times Offset, Malaysia

Contents

introduction

Let's start from the beginning. I grew up with baking. My mother was an excellent cook and her cakes turned out perfectly. I used to perch on a stool by her side as she cooked. I remember licking the creamy cake mixture from a wooden spoon while she lifted her mouth-watering cakes from the oven, aromas of fresh butter and eggs wafting through the house. She drew most of her recipes from the *Radiation New World Cookery Book*, a 1950's book of excellent recipes with short, concise and easy-to-follow methods.

After such a wonderful childhood of being cosseted with these fine tea-time treats, it was little surprise that I too developed an instinctive passion for the sweeter things in life. Little cafés with the simple comforts of warm, sugary doughnuts and rock cakes were my favourite haunts. As a young art student on my first trip to Paris, I rejoiced in the Quartier Montorgueil with its elegant pâtisseries, hidden cafés and bakeries that filled the pavements with inviting smells. This is where I tasted my first madeleines. Their perfect shell-shaped pattern, dipped in fresh pink fondant, seemed like heaven on earth.

It was some years later, while working as a magazine designer in London, that my talent for baking blossomed. A recipe for breakfast buns caught my attention and was enough to lure me into the kitchen and, to my huge surprise, the little golden buns rose to a gentle fluffy peak and tasted wonderful. It was in this moment of culinary nirvana that I realized that I could cook and I am sure that the success of those tempting bakes were the early beginnings of my transition from a career in art to a career in cooking.

Not long after becoming a young wife and mother living in the country, I was ornamenting pie crusts with fancy scalloped edgings, cooking up preserves and rustling up home-made buttery biscuits. It seemed the most obvious thing to do with so many wonderful ingredients around me: fresh, yellow butter from the Jersey cow two fields away, free-range eggs from the local farm and a wealth of wild fruit. But as well as these familiar ingredients, I was searching out exotic and unusual ones to create new and exciting flavour combinations.

Some years later, with more freedom and a desire to travel and search out new ideas, I visited New York where I was introduced to my first real American muffin. Next came the spice markets of North Africa and a myriad of bustling little cafés in the souks selling honey-soaked pastries layered with nuts with the sweet and evocative fragrances of distilled roses or scented orange blossom. There were other culinary holiday favourites: Sweden offered pale buttermilk bakes and Italy showcased amaretti biscuits, fragrant with almonds that seemed to crop up with great frequency in every café or back street restaurant I entered.

I took some of these culinary jewels home with me to adapt and recreate in my own kitchen to make a warming collection of recipes, some of which you'll find in this book. More often than not I find that the best cakes are those baked with quality ingredients. Always try to use the freshest ingredients wherever possible as these will give your bakes a really special home-made aroma. I hope that you enjoy making these recipes as much as I do and that many will become your own personal favourites.

the essential baking kit

The baker and pastry maker is as good as his or her tools and will need a selection of brushes, cake tins and cutters to make melt-in-the-mouth pastries and perfect bakes. This section outlines the basic kitchen gadgets required for perfect baking, along with recipes for making your own sweet accessories, fondants, icings and pastries.

measuring spoons

Exact spoon measurements are vital in baking so make sure you stick to the exact measurements for each recipe.

baking trays or sheets, cake tins and cooling racks

Choose heavy gauge iron baking trays and sheets that do not buckle as these will last longer.

Always use a loose-bottomed tin – unless for very liquidy cake mixes, as it makes it easier for turning out cakes. Ordinary cake tins will need greasing with a little butter and require a lining of baking parchment cut to size. Large, heavy fruit cakes that require extensive baking need to be lined at the sides and the base to protect them from over-browning during prolonged cooking.

Look out for the slimmer loaf tins that sometimes come with collapsible sides. These are ideal for sticky cakes and chocolate cakes. Non-stick cake tins don't need lining unless you're baking a large cake that needs prolonged cooking. However, they do need to be handled with reverence as their surface scratches easily.

Cooling racks are essential to allow the steaming moisture from the cakes to escape more easily.

special baking tins

For tarte Tatin, you should ideally buy a special tarte Tatin tin with sloping sides. A heavy gauge one is best, as Tatins are generally cooked on the hob as well as in the oven. Tins are available in good kitchenware shops. Otherwise you could use a small 20-cm (8-in) frying pan with sloping sides and metal handles.

Muffin tins have deeper and larger holes than the standard bun tin. They come in sheets of 12 holes in metal or non-stick. You can also bake the muffins in paper cases set inside the holes of the muffin tin which is what is suggested in all the muffin recipes in this book. Look out for Texas muffin pans double the size of the ordinary individual muffin tin to make extra large muffins.

Madeleine trays usually contain 12 or 16 holes, each with a shell-shaped impression that gives a pretty shape to the rich, buttery batter as it bakes. They also come in mini sizes for petits fours.

SPOON MEASUREMENTS
1 tsp = 1 level tsp
Lightly-rounded tsp = 1¼ tsps
Rounded tsp = 1½ tsps
1 dssp = 2 level tsps
1 tbsp = 4 level tsps

LOAF TINS SIZES
½ lb (capacity ¾ pt)
1 lb (capacity 1½ pts)
2 lbs (capacity 3 pts)

Roulade or Swiss roll tins are oblong, shallow tins made in heavy gauge tin or silver anodized metal. The ideal size for a roulade tin is 40 x 25 cm (16 x 10 in) but these may not fit smaller ovens so 35 x 25 cm (14 x 10 in) is fairly standard. If you can't find one, a standard oven roasting tray, although a little deep, is fine. Swiss roll tins are a fairly standard size, usually 20 x 30 cm (8 x 12 in) and 2.5-cm (1-in) deep.

baking beans

Baking beans for baking blind are made of porcelain or metal and are available from good kitchen shops. Dried beans work just as well and can be kept and used time and again. Some cooks use rice or broken macaroni, both of which keep indefinitely.

cutters

Cutters come in various shapes and sizes. A lattice roller cutter is a gadget devised for cutting and giving a pretty open latticework pattern to sheets of rolled-out pastry.

A graded set of plain or fluted tinned steel biscuit cutters are essential for making biscuits, pastry decorations and scones.

A canella is a type of zester that cuts fine spaghetti-like strands from hard skinned citrus fruits which you can use to decorate the tops of lemon- or orange-flavoured cakes and muffins.

paper

Baking parchment is used throughout the book, but look out for a baking parchment almost like a canvas-textured fabric which you can wipe clean and re-use. Kitchen foil can be added to a baking sheet and very lightly greased with butter if you need a substitute for parchment when baking meringues. Double folded and placed over the cake towards the end of baking, it will protect the top of a cake from over-browning. However, many cooks still swear by using a double-folded piece of baking parchment to loosely cover the tops of cakes to keep them appetisingly golden towards the end of baking.

Wax paper muffin cases are convenient for easy release. Double the cases for neater shaped cakes or treble them for strength if cooking them free-standing on a baking sheet. There are also ready-made paper liners for round cake tins and loaf-shaped cakes which are particularly good when making sticky cakes and sweet breads.

sweet accessories and pastries

Below are some recipes for cake fillings, coverings and glazes used frequently in baking, along with a selection of melt-in-the-mouth pastries, the foundation to many wonderful pies and tarts that can be as delicious and imaginative as their fillings.

egg glaze

1 egg yolk
Pinch of salt
1–2 tbsps milk

Beat all the ingredients together with a fork until well amalgamated. Use to brush over pastry before baking to ensure a rich, golden colour.

apricot glaze

200 g/7 oz apricot jam (jelly)
115 g/4 oz/$\frac{1}{2}$ cup caster (superfine) sugar
75 ml/2 fl oz/$\frac{1}{4}$ cup water
1 tbsp lemon juice

Boil all the ingredients together until rich and syrupy. Press the mixture through a sieve and, while it is still warm and fluid, brush over the top and sides of the cake.

red glaze

175 g/6 oz/$\frac{3}{4}$ cup redcurrant jelly
1 tbsp water

Warm the jelly and water gently in a pan on a low heat and stir until melted but do not whisk or the glaze will cloud. Cook for a maximum of two minutes or the glaze will darken. Use warm and fluid, as with the yellow glaze.

coloured sugars

Coloured sugars are used to add colour and extra sweetness to biscuits and cakes. Add four or five drops of any natural food colouring to a glass jam jar containing 55 g/2 oz/$\frac{1}{4}$ cup of caster (superfine) sugar and shake vigorously for two to three minutes until the sugar is evenly coloured.

vanilla cream

284 ml/9$\frac{1}{2}$ fl oz/1$\frac{1}{4}$ cups double (heavy) cream
2 tsps caster (superfine) sugar
1 tsp pure vanilla extract, or
 pure vanilla bean paste

Add all the ingredients to a mixing bowl and beat into just firm peaks (the cream will thicken a little more as you pipe it). This classic cream filling, sometimes called Chantilly cream, works well for a multitude of cakes, roulades and éclairs.

banoffi cream

1 large tin of condensed milk
248 ml/9$\frac{1}{2}$ fl oz/1$\frac{1}{4}$ cups cream, whipped
 to the soft peak stage

Pierce two small holes in the can's lid and stand it in a large pan of boiling water, ensuring the top of the tin is above water level. Leave on a gentle rolling boil for two hours, keeping an eye on the water level, then carefully remove from the water. Leave it to cool for half and hour then open the can, covering it first with a tea cloth. Scoop the contents into a bowl and whisk it vigorously with the cream until smooth. Alternatively, banoffi toffee can be bought ready-made in jars.

raspberry buttercream

100 g/3½ oz/scant 1 stick butter, softened
350 g/12 oz/2½ cups icing (confectioner's)
   sugar, double sifted
1½ tbsps lemon juice
3 tbsps of home-made raspberry jam (jelly)
A little water

Beat the softened butter with the icing sugar in a large mixing bowl, gradually adding the lemon juice, jam and enough water to make a soft mixture that holds its shape. Use to fill a sponge cake or spread thickly over a roulade.

citrus zest icing

225 g/8 oz/1½ cups icing (confectioner's)
   sugar, double sifted
3 tbsps lemon juice
Zest of 1 lime, grated
Zest of 1 lemon, grated
Zest of 1 orange, grated

Add the icing sugar to a large mixing bowl and vigorously stir in the lemon juice until the consistency is smooth and shiny. Finally, add the grated fruit zest and mix thoroughly. Try lime, orange or lemon, or all three together to add a fresh zestiness to a variety of bakes. Drizzle over your favourite bakes and allow to set.

crème fraîche frosting

1 carton crème fraîche
Juice of 1 lemon
Zest of 2 lemons
Icing (confectioner's) sugar, double sifted
   (enough to thicken the icing into soft peaks)

In the bowl of an electric mixer, whisk all the ingredients together at a low to medium speed for about three minutes until a thick and creamy consistency is achieved. Cover and chill for at least one hour before using.

lemon curd

3 large egg yolks and 1 egg white
55 g/2 oz/½ stick butter
175 g/6 oz/scant 1 cup caster (superfine) sugar
Juice and finely grated rind of 1 large
   unwaxed lemon

Add the ingredients to a small saucepan and set over a moderate heat, stirring until the mixture just begins to thicken. Remove from the heat immediately and pour into a clean jam jar. Seal and store in the fridge for up to one month.

fondant

250 g/8½ oz/1¼ cups sugar
150 ml/5 fl oz/⅔ cup water
1 tbsp liquid glucose (available from
   larger supermarkets)

Mix all the ingredients in a saucepan and bring to a soft boil at 116–118°C (241–244°F) on a sugar thermometer, or until a blob of syrup holds its shape. Brush a large marble slab with cold water and pour the syrup onto it. Cool for one minute until it begins to thicken. Use a palette knife to work the syrup, scraping and folding it over repeatedly until it is a thick, opaque paste. As the sugar cools and crystallizes, it forms a white crunchy mixture. Work this mixture with your fingertips, kneading small chunks of it into a smooth paste. Well wrapped in polythene, these small chunks will store in a dry place for up to a year. Alternatively, fondant can be bought in powder form from specialist cake makers. Ideally, fondant should be allowed to mature for a day before it is used as a coating. To use, heat enough small pieces in a bowl over hot but not boiling water until they melt.

To colour fondant, infuse a high quality food paste colouring. These are so intense that you may only need a tiny speck to tint it. For chocolate or coffee fondant, add cocoa, melted chocolate or coffee essence to the fondant.

marzipan

225 g/8 oz/2 cups almonds, finely ground
110 g/4 oz/scant 1 cup icing (confectioner's) sugar, sifted
110 g/4 oz/½ cup caster (superfine) sugar
Few drops vanilla extract
2 tsps rum or brandy
2 large egg whites, whisked until foamy

Place the almonds, two types of sugar, vanilla and rum or brandy in a mixing bowl. Add enough whisked egg white to make a moist ball of paste. Knead until perfectly smooth and free of cracks. Keep covered in plastic wrap in the fridge until required. Well wrapped, it will keep for several months.

You can mould marzipan into pretty shapes and use them to decorate the tops of cakes. Gently knead the paste on a work surface lightly dusted with icing sugar until smooth and free of cracks. Divide it into small portions and press each one into your chosen decorative mould, level the top and scrape away any excess marzipan with a sharp knife. If using a soft, rubber mould, demould the shapes immediately. If the mould is made of rigid clear plastic, freeze the marzipan until it is hard then press the tip of a knife between the marzipan and the mould to prise it out. Marzipan bought from a good cake supplier is usually of good

enough quality and slightly better for moulding than home-made marzipan.

stencilled icing sugar patterns

Add a last minute dusting of icing (confectioner's) sugar to the surface of a cake or tart. A simple criss-cross pattern can be made by placing strips of paper 1–2-cm (¼–¾-in) wide, so that they overlap at regular intervals to make a snowy white criss-cross decoration like latticework across the top of a cake or tart. For a spider web pattern, lay a round wire cooling rack on top of a cake and sift over a fine layer of icing sugar then carefully lift off the rack. Otherwise, cut out decorative flower or leaf shapes from a sheet of paper or baking parchment and remember that the shapes you cut out will be the areas to be covered with icing sugar.

sweet pastry

175 g/6 oz/1½ cups plain (all-purpose) flour
100 g/4 oz/1 stick butter
Pinch of salt
50 g/2 oz/generous ¼ cup icing (confectioner's) sugar, sifted
Rind of ¼ lemon, grated
½ large egg, beaten

Sift the flour onto a work surface, make a well in the centre and into it place the butter, salt, sugar, lemon rind and egg. Draw the fingers of one hand together and lightly and quickly combine the ingredients in the well with your fingertips until the mixture is soft and blended. Gradually draw in the flour from around the edges and, using the same fingertip movement, combine the ingredients to form a crumb-like mixture. Gather together and lightly press the moist crumbs into a soft ball. Gently knead the dough on a lightly-floured surface until smooth, ensuring you do not overwork the dough. Wrap in a plastic bag and chill for 2 hours before using.

rich sweet pastry

225 g/8 oz/2 cups plain (all-purpose) flour
115 g/4 oz/1 stick butter, cubed
90 g/3½ oz/½ cup caster (superfine) sugar
Large pinch of salt
1½ tsps vanilla extract
3 large egg yolks

Sift the flour onto a board and make an open well in the centre. Into it place the butter, sugar, salt, vanilla and egg yolks. Draw the fingertips of one hand together and, lightly and quickly, work the ingredients in the well with a bird-like pecking motion until the mixture resembles scrambled eggs. Gradually, draw in the flour and, using the same finger movement, quickly combine the remaining ingredients to form a crumb-like mixture. Gather together and lightly press the moist crumbs into a soft ball. Lightly knead the dough by pushing it away from you with the heel of your hand and drawing it back four to five times until the pastry is smooth. Wrap in a plastic bag and chill for 1 hour. Knead lightly before using to make it smooth.

mascarpone and soured cream pastry

175 g/6 oz/1½ sticks butter, softened
3 tbsps mascarpone
3 tbsps soured (sour) cream
255 g/9 oz/2¼ cups plain (all-purpose) flour, sifted
Pinch of salt

Place the butter, mascarpone and soured cream in a mixing bowl and beat them together. Mix in the sifted flour and salt with a palette knife. Finish off lightly with your fingertips to make a soft, moist dough. Wrap in a plastic bag and chill for 45 to 60 minutes before using.

orange and cardamom pastry

225 g/8 oz/2 cups plain (all-purpose) flour
Pinch of salt
8 green cardamom pods
115 g/4 oz/1 stick butter, cubed
90 g/3½ oz/½ cup caster (superfine) sugar
3 large egg yolks
Rind of 1 orange, grated

Sift the flour and salt onto a board and make an open well in the centre. Crush the cardamom pods to release the small black seeds. Place the seeds in a small plastic bag and crush them with a rolling pin to make a fine powder. Shake the powdered seeds through a sieve and sprinkle them over the flour. Place the butter, sugar, egg yolks and orange zest in the well. With the fingers of one hand held together, work lightly and quickly until the mixture resembles scrambled eggs. Draw the flour into the mixture until it forms large, moist crumbs. Lightly knead the dough by pushing it away from you with the heel of your hand and drawing it back four to five times until the pastry is smooth. Wrap in a plastic bag and chill for 45 minutes before using.

brisée pastry

225 g/8 oz/2 cups plain (all-purpose) flour
½ tsp salt
1 tsp caster (superfine) sugar
115 g/4 oz/1 stick butter
2 large egg yolks
3½ tbsps cold water

Sift the flour and salt onto a work surface and make a well in the centre. Into it place the sugar, butter, egg yolks and water. Using your fingertips, lightly and quickly work the ingredients in the well with a bird-like pecking motion until the mixture resembles scrambled eggs. Draw in the flour to form a crumb-like mixture then bring the mixture together with your hands to form a soft moist dough. Wrap in a plastic bag and chill for 2 hours.

puff pastry

Because all the ingredients for puff pastry have to be kept chilled, it is recommened you don't make it on a hot day or when the kitchen is warm from other cooking. The whole operation could be ruined if the butter is allowed to become too soft. Any leftover rolled-out pastry can be used to gain the same puffiness if you press the scraps together side to side (never back into a ball) so the layers are maintained.

200 g/7 oz/1^2/$_3$ cups plain (all-purpose) flour
½ tsp salt
200 g/7 oz/2 sticks butter, chilled
5 tbsps iced water mixed with 1 tsp lemon juice

1   Sift the flour and salt into a large mixing bowl and add about a quarter of the butter, cutting it roughly into the flour with a knife. Return the remaining butter to the fridge. Mix with your fingertips until it resembles fine breadcrumbs, then mix to a firm but moist dough with the cold water and lemon juice. Wrap in a plastic bag and chill for 30 minutes.

2   Take the remaining butter out of the fridge and place it between two pieces of baking parchment. Pound it, pressing it into a 10-cm (4-in) square about 2 cm

(¾ in) deep. At this stage the butter must not be too soft or too hard. Ideally, it should be of a similar texture to the dough so that they can be easily rolled together.

3   Unwrap the dough and roll it into a 15-cm (6-in) square and place the butter diagonally over the centre of the pastry. Pull up the four corners of the dough to cover the butter and use a rolling pin to press down the seams to seal them. Place the dough in a plastic bag and refrigerate for 20 minutes. Remove the dough from the fridge and place it on a floured board, seam-side up.

4   Roll out the dough into a rectangle, three times as long as it is wide, always rolling away from you and not from side to side. Keep the edges and corners square, if necessary gently easing them out with your fingertips. Fold the top one-third down and the bottom one-third up to make three layers. Use a lightly floured rolling pin to press the edges and seams gently together, then turn the dough 90 degrees to your right so that it opens like a book. This is called a turn. Wrap and chill for 30 minutes.

5   Roll out again into a rectangle three times as long as it is wide, fold the top one-third down and the bottom one-third up to make three layers. Use a lightly floured rolling pin to press the edges and seams gently together, and turn to 90 degrees. Wrap and chill for 30 minutes.

6   Repeat steps 4 and 5 twice more, including the chilling each time. Keep it well wrapped and chilled if you are not going to use it straight away. It will keep in the fridge for two to three days, or you can freeze it too. Defrost it in the fridge slowly overnight, not at room temperature.

cakes and cheesecakes

Few customs give greater satisfaction than the old fashioned one of afternoon tea. My favourite tea-time experience is relaxing by an open fire with a pot of Earl Grey and a delicious stack of crumbly cherry cakes, a Victoria sponge topped with lemon icing or perhaps a rich slice of fruit cake to feast my eyes on. It is my firm conviction that no commercial brand of unknown provenance stands a chance next to a home-baked cake made in my own kitchen.

Whether it be a modest madeira or a rich fruit celebration cake, I always buy the best ingredients that I can afford as the quality of the ingredients speaks volumes in the final flavour: good fresh butter – farmhouse or French if it is available – fresh free-range eggs, pure vanilla bean paste or even better seeds scraped from the pod itself, freshly ground spices and zest fresh-grated from firm, ripe citrus fruits.

The right sized tins and accurate measurements are also important for producing good cakes that are well-risen and appetisingly golden. The rest is chemistry and creativity. If a cake mixture works for you, swap around the ingredients; for example, the Cranberry and clementine muffin cake would work equally well with plums and walnuts, apples and blackberries, or damsons and quince jelly. But above all, have fun and set aside a morning for baking. I guarantee it is the greatest de-stresser of all time.

pear and quince cake

This delicious autumn cake works equally well served warm as a pudding. I usually add one-third of quinces to pears. Keep some of the pear slices complete with stalks and pips to add to the top of the cake mixture before baking for a pretty autumnal look.

SERVES 9

FOR THE FRUIT
900 g/2 lb ripe but firm pears
  and quinces
  (see recipe introduction)
Lemon juice
40 g/1½ oz/¼ stick butter
55 g/2 oz/generous ¼ cup
  caster (superfine) sugar

FOR THE CAKE BATTER
55g/2oz/½ stick butter
175 g/6 oz/scant 1 cup caster
  (superfine) sugar
2 large eggs
1 tbsp milk
1 tsp vanilla extract or pure
  vanilla bean paste
1 tbsp rum or brandy
175 g/6 oz/1½ cups plain
  (all-purpose) flour

1 tsp baking powder
Pinch of salt

FOR THE GLAZE
1 tbsp quince jelly or
  quince jam (preserves)
25 g/1 oz/1½ tbsps caster
  (superfine) sugar
2 tbsps water
1–2 tbsps rum or brandy

1 Preheat the oven to 180°C (350°F). To prepare the fruit, peel and cut the pears and quinces into halves lengthways and remove the cores then cut each piece lengthways again into four slices. Brush with a little lemon juice to prevent them from browning.

2 Heat the butter in a frying pan and add the fruit slices. Sprinkle over the sugar and cook them in their juices for about 10 to 15 minutes, turning the pieces frequently until golden on all sides. Cook a few pear halves with their stalks and pips and reserve them to decorate the top of the cake.

3 To make the cake batter, beat the butter and sugar together until it looks light and crumbly. Add the eggs one at a time and continue to beat until creamy. Gradually beat in the milk, vanilla and rum or brandy until the cake batter is smooth. Sift the flour, baking powder and salt into the mix and stir lightly until well combined but do not over mix. Add the pear and quince slices to the cake batter and spoon it into a buttered and floured square 23-cm (9-in) tin lined at the base and sides with baking parchment. Add the reserved pear halves with the small stalks on top of the batter, (they will sink in to the mixture more during baking). Bake for 50 minutes.

4 To make the glaze, dissolve the quince jelly or jam and sugar in the water and boil for 2 minutes without stirring. Stir in the rum or brandy and, while it is still hot, brush it thickly over the surface of the cake. Eat warm or cold.

quince and chocolate coils

Quince jelly and crushed dark (semisweet) chocolate make a sweet piquant filling to these unusual coil-shaped pastries. Use 00 Italian flour, available from a good delicatessen, as you need a fairly robust pastry that holds its shape.

MAKES 10

FOR THE PASTRY
225 g/8 oz/2 cups 00 Italian
   flour
Pinch of salt
140 g/5 oz/1¼ stick butter,
   cubed
2 tsps caster (superfine) sugar
1 large egg yolk, mixed with
   2 tbsps water

FOR THE FILLING
225 g/8 oz/1 cup quince jelly
55 g (2 oz) dark (semisweet)
   chocolate, cut into slivers
Egg glaze (see page 9)
2–3 tbsps granulated sugar

1 Sift the flour and salt into a mixing bowl, then add the cubed butter to the flour. Stir in the sugar. Using your fingertips, rub the mixture quickly and lightly until it resembles fine breadcrumbs, then mix in enough of the egg and water mixture to make a soft moist paste.

2 Dust the work surface with flour and knead the paste for 1 minute. Refrigerate for 10 minutes so that the pastry dough is chilled but still fairly malleable.

3 Dust the work surface with flour and roll the dough thinly into a 30-cm (12-in) square. Make a horizontal cut half way across the whole square then make four vertical cuts across to make 10 strips measuring 15 x 6 cm (6 x 2½ in).

4 Preheat the oven to 190°C (375°F). To make the filling, combine the jelly and the chocolate. Spread the mixture along the centre of each strip and roll up lengthways into a sausage. Cut the end pieces of the sausages at an angle, dab on a little egg glaze and gently press down to seal. Brush the whole surface of the sausages with more egg glaze, roll them up into coils and press together. Using a palette knife, transfer the coiled shapes onto a baking sheet lightly greased with butter. Sprinkle each coil with ¼ teaspoon of sugar, and bake for 12 minutes, until the pastry is crisp and lightly golden. Leave to cool completely before serving.

gooseberry hill muffin cake

You can use a mixture of fresh fruits or just gooseberries for this mouth-watering recipe. You could make muffins instead of a cake, just follow the method for Raspberry and fig muffins on page 74.

MAKES 1 CAKE OR 10 MUFFINS

FOR THE FRUIT
140 g/5 oz/generous ½ cup gooseberries, or Cox's apples sliced with gooseberries
1½ tbsps golden caster (superfine) sugar
1 tbsp elderflower cordial, (optional)

FOR THE CAKE MIX
225 g/8 oz/2 cups plain (all-purpose) flour
2 rounded tsps baking powder
Pinch of salt
140 g/5 oz/¾ cup golden (superfine) caster sugar
85 g/3 oz/⅓ cup melted butter

½ tsp vanilla extract or pure vanilla bean paste
1 large egg, lightly beaten
284 ml/9½ fl oz/1¼ cups buttermilk

Icing (confectioner's) sugar, to dust

1 Start by preparing the fruit. Fruit on its own can be slightly acidic so lay the fruit out in a single layer on a plate and evenly sprinkle the sugar over it with the elderflower cordial, if using, about 30 minutes before baking.

2 Preheat the oven to 180°C (350°F). To make the cake mix, sift the dry ingredients into a large mixing bowl and mix thoroughly. In a separate bowl, mix the warm, melted butter, vanilla, egg and the buttermilk together. Make a well in the centre of the dry ingredients and pour in the buttermilk mixture. Fold it in gently until nearly blended, making sure not to over mix.

3 Gently fold in half the fruits and the sugary juices to the mix. Spoon the mixture into a lightly buttered 23-cm (9-in) round loose-bottomed tin and sprinkle the remaining fruit on top which will sink a little into the cake mixture as it bakes.

4 Bake for 30 minutes but check several minutes before. If the centre of the cake feels springy to the touch it is ready. Serve, lightly dusted with icing sugar. It stores well for three to four days well wrapped and stored in an airtight tin.

clementine and cranberry muffin cake

This amount of mixture can also make 10 individual muffins. Divide the mixture and baked fruit equally between the muffin paper cases set inside the holes of the tin. You will need to prepare the clementines two hours before you start making the cake.

SERVES 8 TO 10

FOR THE FRUIT
2 clementines
85 g/3 oz/scant ½ cup kumquats, halved
140 g/5 oz/1½ cups fresh cranberries
2 tbsps redcurrant jelly
70 g/2½ oz/generous ¼ cup caster (superfine) sugar
25 g (1 oz) butter

FOR THE CAKE MIX
225 g/8 oz/2 cups plain (all-purpose) flour
2 rounded tsps baking powder
Pinch salt
140 g/5 oz/¾ cup caster (superfine) sugar
85 g/3 oz/⅓ cup melted butter
1 large egg

284 ml/10 fl oz/1¼ cups buttermilk

Icing (confectioner's) sugar, to dust
Lightly sweetened crème fraîche, to serve

1 Add the whole clementines, unpeeled, to a medium-size saucepan and cover with boiling water. Cover with a lid and simmer for 2 hours over a low to moderate heat, checking the water levels every now and again. Remove the clementines from the heat and when they have cooled, split them open and remove the pips. Liquidize them to a smooth, orange-coloured purée and set aside.

2 Preheat the oven to 180°C (375°F). In a flat, oven-proof container, mix the halved kumquats, cranberries, redcurrant jelly and sugar and dot over with the butter. Bake for 8 minutes, until the juices start to run and the fruit looks glossy. Baste a couple of times to amalgamate the fruit, then remove from the oven and leave the sweetened glossy fruit to cool in the syrup.

3 To make the cake mix, sift the dry ingredients into a large mixing bowl. In a smaller bowl, mix in the cooled melted butter with the egg, buttermilk and puréed clementine. Make a well in the centre of the dry ingredients. Pour in the clementine and buttermilk mixture and fold it in gently until nearly blended. Fold in half the braised fruit making sure not to over mix the mixture.

4 Lightly butter a 23-cm (9-in) round loose-bottomed tin 4-cm (1½-in) deep. Spoon the mixture into the tin and sprinkle the remaining braised fruit on top. Bake for 30 minutes. When slightly cooled, turn out onto a wire cooling rack. Serve cut into wedges with a thick dusting of icing sugar and a spoonful of lightly sweetened crème fraîche. The cake will store for up four days in an airtight tin.

organic lemon and lime drizzle cake

A sharp citrus icing enhanced with flecks of lemon and lime zest is the integral part of this delicious sponge cake. Serve it freshly baked and freshly iced when it is at its best.

SERVES 8

FOR THE CAKE MIX
2 large organic eggs
115 g/4 oz/½ cup organic caster (superfine) sugar
100 ml/3½ fl oz/½ cup double (heavy) organic cream

Zest of 1 organic lemon, grated
1 tbsp organic lemon juice
115 g/4 oz/1 cup organic self-raising (self-rising) flour
1 tsp baking powder
50 g/1¾ oz/½ stick organic butter, melted

FOR THE LEMON AND LIME ICING
225 g/8 oz/1½ cups icing (confectioner's) sugar, double sifted
3 tbsps organic lemon juice
2 tsps organic lime juice
1 tsp organic lemon zest
1 tsp organic lime zest

1 Preheat the oven to 180°C (350°F). Lightly beat the eggs with the sugar. Beat the cream into the egg mixture for about 1 minute, then add the lemon zest and juice. Fold in the sifted flour and baking powder then fold in the melted butter.

2 Three-quarters fill a lightly buttered 450-g (1-lb) loaf tin lined at the base with baking parchment and stand it on a baking tray in the centre of the oven. Bake for about 40 to 45 minutes until well risen and golden. Test by lightly pressing the cake with your fingers, the sponge should lightly spring back. Leave to cool on a wire cooling rack.

3 To make the icing, sift the icing sugar into a mixing bowl and stir in the lemon and lime juices until the consistency is smooth and shiny then stir in the zests. Pour the icing over the cake, evenly coating the surface. Serve freshly baked and freshly iced.

citrus syrup cake

Unusually, this cake is made without flour. After it is baked, the cake is pricked all over and soaked with a heavy citrus-scented syrup. Serve with fresh berries lightly dusted with icing sugar and a scoop of vanilla ice cream.

SERVES 8

FOR THE CAKE MIX
2 clementines
6 large eggs
225 g/8 oz/generous 1 cup caster (superfine) sugar
225 g/8 oz/1$\frac{1}{2}$ cups ground almonds

FOR THE CITRUS SYRUP
350 g/12 oz/1$\frac{3}{4}$ cups caster (superfine) sugar
Zest of 1 clementine, cut into fine strips
Juice of $\frac{3}{4}$ lemon

Fresh berries and vanilla ice cream, to serve
Icing (confectioner's) sugar, to dust

1 To make the cake mix, put the whole clementines, unpeeled, into a pan and cover with boiling water. Bring to the boil then simmer for about 2 hours keeping a check on the water level. Remove the clementines from the heat and when they have cooled, split them open and remove the pips. Liquidize them to a smooth, orange-coloured purée. Set aside.

2 Preheat the oven to 160°C (325°F). Whisk the eggs and sugar together until well combined, then stir in the ground almonds and the puréed fruit. Pour the mixture into a lightly buttered 23-cm (9-in) round loose-bottomed tin and bake for 45 minutes until firm to the touch.

3 Meanwhile, make the citrus syrup. Slowly dissolve the sugar over a medium heat in 250 ml/9 fl oz/generous 1 cup water. Add the strips of fruit zest and the lemon juice and bring to the boil. Reduce the heat and simmer for 2 to 3 minutes until the liquid thinly coats the back of a spoon.

4 Allow the cake to cool in the tin, then with the prongs of a fork, prick the surface of the cake and pour over the warm syrup, spoonfuls at a time, until it is all used up. Serve with fresh berries and a scoop of ice scream or store in an airtight tin until required. It keeps well for up to four days if well wrapped.

max's wild berry cheesecake

This simple no-cook cheesecake has a delicious sweet but sharp filling. In the absence of fresh blackberries, try raspberries or strawberries which look lovely in summer when you can add a few fresh fruit leaves lightly dusted with icing sugar on top of the cheesecake just before serving.

SERVES 6

FOR THE BISCUIT BASE
85 g (3 oz) digestive biscuits (graham crackers)
55 g/2 oz/scant ½ cup demerara (raw brown) sugar
55 g/3 oz/¾ stick butter, melted

FOR THE CHEESE MIXTURE
225 g/8 oz/1 cup rich cream cheese
225 g/8 oz/1 cup fresh curd cheese
1 large egg, separated
55 g/2 oz/scant ¼ cup caster (superfine) sugar
160 ml/5 fl oz/⅔ cup natural yoghurt

Rind of 1 small orange, grated
Juice of 1 lemon
1 sachet (envelope) powdered gelatine (gelatin)
225 g/8 oz/scant 1 cup fresh, ripe blackberries

Icing (confectioner's) sugar, to dust

1   Start by preparing the biscuit base. Crush the biscuits in a food processor until they resemble coarse breadcrumbs. You could also place the biscuits in a plastic bag and crush them with a rolling pin. Transfer the crumbs to a mixing bowl and stir in the sugar and warm, melted butter. Press the crumbs into the base of an 18-cm (7-in) round loose-bottomed tin 5 cm (2 in) deep and level with the back of a large spoon. Leave to set in the fridge.

2   To make the cheese mixture, beat the cream and curd cheeses in a large mixing bowl until smooth, then add the egg yolk, sugar, yoghurt and orange rind. Continue to beat until the mixture is smooth. In a separate bowl, whisk the egg white until stiff and set aside.

3   Add the lemon juice to a small bowl and sprinkle over the gelatine. Leave until completely soaked for 3 to 4 minutes, then stand the cup in a small bowl of hot water until dissolved.

4   Stir the liquid gelatine into the cheese mixture, then gently fold in the egg white. Remove the tin from the fridge, pour in the mixture and smooth the surface with a palette knife. Chill for at least four hours until set, then carefully unmould. Decorate with blackberries and a light dusting of icing sugar.

marrons glacés and ginger cheesecake

You can buy preserved marrons glacés (candied chestnuts) in a jar and use them and the syrup to make a luxurious addition to this rich ginger-based cheesecake. You can, if you prefer, keep the flavour all ginger by adding paper-thin slices of stem (preserved) ginger to the topping instead of the marrons glacés.

SERVES 8

FOR THE BISCUIT BASE
85 g/3 oz ginger biscuits (cookies)
85 g/3 oz digestive biscuits (graham crackers)
25 g/1 oz/¼ cup demerara (raw brown) sugar
55 g/2 oz/½ stick butter, melted

FOR THE CHEESE MIXTURE
225 g/½ lb/1 cup cream cheese
225 g/½ lb/1 cup curd cheese
160 ml/5 fl oz/⅔ cup natural yoghurt
1 large egg, separated
½ tsp powdered ginger
1½ tbsps clear, runny honey
1½ tbsps ginger syrup from the stem (preserved) ginger

1 tbsp mandarin- or orange-flavoured liqueur, (optional)
2 pieces stem (preserved) ginger, very finely chopped
1 sachet (envelope) powdered gelatine (gelatin)

4–5 marrons glacés (candied chestnuts), halved, or 4–5 pieces stem (preserved) ginger, to decorate

1 Start by preparing the biscuit base. Crush the two types of biscuit (the cookies and the graham crackers) in a food processor until they resemble coarse breadcrumbs. Transfer the crumbs to a mixing bowl and stir in the sugar and warm, melted butter. Press the crumbs into the base of a lightly buttered 20-cm (8-inch) round loose-bottomed tin and level with the back of a large spoon. Leave to set in the fridge.

2 To make the cheese mixture, beat the cream and curd cheeses in a large mixing bowl until smooth, then add the yoghurt, egg yolk, ginger, honey, ginger syrup and liqueur, if using. Stir in the chopped stem ginger.

3 Put the gelatine in a cup and, with a fork, whisk in 1 tablespoon of boiling water. Place the base of the cup in hot water until the gelatine has completely dissolved. In a separate mixing bowl, whisk the egg white until stiff and set aside.

4 Stir the melted gelatine into the mixture, then gently fold in the egg white. Remove the tin from the fridge, pour in the mixture and smooth the surface with a palette knife. Chill for at least 4 hours until set, then carefully unmould. Serve in slices decorated with the marrons glacés and a drizzle of syrup, or substitute with slivers of stem ginger and syrup.

raspberry and pina colada cheesecake

This luxurious cheesecake with its fine Winward Island flavours and creamy mousse-like texture is delicate enough to end the most elegant meal. You can substitute raspberries for fresh pineapple sliced very thinly.

SERVES 8

FOR THE BISCUIT BASE
100 g (3½ oz) digestive biscuits (graham crackers)
25 g/1 oz/¼ cup demerara (raw brown) sugar
40 g/1½ oz/½ stick butter, melted

FOR THE CHEESE MIXTURE
3 large eggs
100 g/3½ oz/½ cup caster (superfine) sugar
200 g/7 oz/scant 1 cup soft cream cheese
3 leaves of gelatine (gelatin)
2 tbsps pineapple juice
50 ml/2 fl oz/¼ cup Malibu liqueur

175 ml/6 fl oz/⅔ cup double (heavy) cream
100 ml/3½ fl oz/½ cup tinned coconut milk

Fresh raspberries or pineapple slices, to decorate
Icing (confectioner's) sugar, to dust

1 Crush the biscuits in a food processor until they resemble coarse breadcrumbs. Transfer the crumbs to a mixing bowl and stir in the sugar and warm, melted butter. Press the crumbs into the base of a lightly buttered 20-cm (8-in) round loose-bottomed deep tin. Leave to set in the fridge.

2 To make the cheese mixture, whisk the eggs and sugar in a metal mixing bowl set over a pan of hot simmering water, ensuring the bowl does not come into contact with the water. Whisk until the mixture has doubled in volume. Remove the bowl from the pan and continue to whisk until cold, then whisk in the cream cheese.

3 Meanwhile soak the gelatine leaves in cold water for 2 to 3 minutes until soft. In a saucepan, heat the pineapple juice and liqueur. Take the softened gelatine leaves and squeeze out the excess water then dissolve them in the hot but not boiling liqueur and pineapple juice taken off the heat. Add to the cheese mixture.

4 Whip the cream and the coconut milk together until they form soft peaks and fold into the cheese mixture until well combined. Pour over the biscuit base and refrigerate for 4 hours or until set then carefully unmould. Top with fresh raspberries or pineapple slices and add a gentle dusting of icing sugar around the edges.

ginger cake with ginger polka dots

Lemon icing highlights the warm fiery ginger flavours of the cake deliciously. Stem ginger is sold in syrup, and sliced into fine discs, makes an appropriate decoration.

SERVES 12

175 g/6 oz/1½ sticks butter, softened

175 g/6 oz/scant 1 cup golden caster (superfine) sugar

3 large eggs

1½ tbsps black treacle (dark molasses)

2½ tbsps ginger syrup from a stem (preserved) ginger jar

225 g/8 oz/2 cups self-raising (self-rising) flour

2 tsps ground ginger

1–1½ level tbsps ground almonds

2 tbsps single (light) cream

One quantity of citrus zest icing (see page 10)

4–5 pieces of stem (preserved) ginger, to decorate

1 Preheat the oven to 170ºC (325ºF). Cream the butter and sugar together until light and creamy. Gradually beat in the eggs, one by one, beating well between each addition. Fold in the treacle and the ginger syrup. Gradually fold in the flour sifted with the ground ginger. Then fold in the ground almonds, followed by the cream, until well combined.

2 Spoon the cake mix into a buttered 20-cm (8-in) square tin lined at the base with baking parchment and smooth it level. Bake for 40 to 50 minutes, or until the centre of the cake is firm and slightly springy to the touch. Leave to cool slightly in the tin, then turn it out onto a wire cooling rack.

3 When the cake has sufficiently cooled, spread the citrus zest icing over the top, coaxing it towards the edges of the cake with a palette knife. Leave to set. For the polka dot decoration, simply dot the icing with thinly-shaved ginger slices spaced a little apart. Serve cut into squares.

buttermilk and vanilla pound cake

Buttermilk adds a slightly acidic flavour to this simple cake flecked with tiny black vanilla seeds.

SERVES 8

315 g/11 oz/2²/₃ cups plain (all-purpose) flour, sifted
1½ tsps baking powder
½ tsp bicarbonate of soda (baking soda)
Pinch of salt

1 vanilla pod (vanilla bean)
225 ml/8 fl oz/1 cup buttermilk
175 g/6 oz/1½ sticks butter, softened

225 g/8 oz/generous 1 cup caster (superfine) sugar
Zest of 1 lemon
3 large egg yolks
Icing (confectioner's) sugar sifted, to finish

1 Preheat the oven to 180°C (350°F). Sift the flour, baking powder, bicarbonate of soda and salt together into a large mixing bowl. In a separate bowl, split the vanilla pod and gently scrape the seeds into the buttermilk and whisk lightly together. Set aside.

2 Beat the butter then add the sugar and cream them together with the lemon zest. Add the eggs gradually and beat between each addition until the mixture looks light and creamy.

3 Lightly fold the flour mixture alternately with the vanilla scented buttermilk into the creamed egg mixture until lightly combined, finishing with the flour mixture. Spoon the mixture into a lightly buttered 23-cm (9-in) round tin 4 cm (1½ in) deep lined at the base with baking parchment and lightly smooth over the surface with a spatula. Bake for 50 minutes until golden brown, or until a skewer inserted into the cake comes out clean.

tunisian cake

It is important to use a freshly-ground cinnamon stick to add a fresh spicy flavour to this moist, colourful cake made with typically Middle Eastern ingredients.

SERVES 8 TO 10

FOR THE CAKE
115 g/4 oz/1 cup shelled, unsalted pistachio nuts
140 g/5 oz/scant 1 cup ready-soaked apricots
150 g/5½ oz/1½ cups plain (all-purpose) flour
¾ tsp bicarbonate of soda (baking soda)
¼ tsp baking powder
¼ tsp salt

1 tsp freshly ground cinnamon stick
6 large egg yolks
115 g/4 oz/¾ cup soft, light brown sugar
150 g/5½ oz/⅔ cup plain yoghurt
Zest of 1½ oranges, grated
60 ml/2 fl oz/¼ cup olive oil
5 large egg whites
115 g/4 oz/generous ½ cup caster (superfine) sugar

FOR THE APRICOT AND CINNAMON GLAZE
85 g/3 oz/½ cup ready-soaked apricots
1½ tbsps runny honey
Juice of 1 orange
1 large cinnamon stick, broken into halves
Pistachio nuts, to decorate

1 Preheat the oven to 180°C (350°F). Finely chop the pistachios with a knife or whiz them in a food processor and set aside. Finely chop the apricots and set aside with the pistachios.

2 In a mixing bowl, sift the flour with the bicarbonate of soda, baking powder, salt and the ground cinnamon and set aside. In a separate larger bowl, beat the egg yolks with the soft light brown sugar until thick and creamy. Mix in the yoghurt, zest and olive oil then fold in the pistachios, apricots and the flour mixture.

3 Beat the egg whites until stiff, then fold in 1 tbsp of the caster sugar and beat for a further minute. Gently fold the remaining sugar into the meringue mixture then fold lightly into the cake mixture. Pour into a lightly buttered 20-cm (8-in) round loose-bottomed deep cake tin. Bake for 40 to 45 minutes until the cake is firm to the touch, but check after 30 minutes and if the top of the cake is browning too much, cover it with a piece of baking parchment. Leave for 5 minutes to cool in the tin, then turn out onto a wire cooling rack.

4 To make the glaze, add all the glaze ingredients to a saucepan and bring to the boil. Then simmer over a moderate heat for about 6 to 7 minutes until reduced by half. Remove the cinnamon stick from the syrup and place over the centre of the cake. Remove the apricots and set aside (use to decorate the cut cake later) and brush the remaining warm syrup over the top and sides of the cake. Leave the cake to cool completely before slicing. Serve decorated with the reserved apricots or a few pistachios.

summer cake with fondant-dipped redcurrants

Semolina adds a tender crumb and a pretty pale lemon colour to this light, airy sponge cake which is filled with cream flavoured with lemon curd. Redcurrants dipped in a melting fondant complete the picture of this pretty summer cake.

SERVES 8 TO 10

FOR THE CAKE MIX
6 large eggs, separated
225 g/8 oz/generous 1 cup caster (superfine) sugar
Juice and grated rind of 1 unwaxed lemon
115 g/4 oz/1¼ cups fine semolina

25 g/1 oz/¼ cup ground almonds

FOR THE FILLING
160 ml/5 fl oz/⅔ cup double (heavy) cream, whipped
3–4 tbsps lemon curd (see page 10)

Icing (confectioner's) sugar, to dust
Half quantity of fondant (see page 10)
Sprigs of redcurrants and several freshly picked fruit leaves

1 Preheat the oven to 180°C (350°F). Using an electric whisk, beat the egg yolks with the sugar until light and creamy. Add the lemon juice and continue to beat until well combined. Fold in the lemon rind, semolina and almonds with a large spoon.

2 In a separate mixing bowl, whisk the egg whites until stiff then fold them very gently into the egg and semolina mixture. Pour into a lightly buttered and floured 23-cm (9-in) round tin lined at the base with baking parchment and bake for about 30 minutes, until the centre is firm to the touch. Leave to cool slightly then invert on to a wire cooling rack and leave to cool a little before gently peeling away the circle of paper which is now on top, then leave to cool completely.

3 To make the filling, whip the cream until it holds it own shape, then lightly fold in the lemon curd. Using a very sharp long-bladed knife, split the sponge and fill it with the lemon cream. Dust the top with sifted icing sugar, perhaps in a criss-cross pattern (see page 11 for ideas).

4 For the fondant redcurrants, use a couple of redcurrant twigs and dip the fruit into the pale pink fondant. Lay on top of the cake. A few fresh redcurrant leaves lightly dusted around the edges with icing sugar look very pretty indeed.

ALTERNATIVES
Other small fruits, like strawberries, cherries or gooseberries can be used half dipped into liquid icing and left to set on non-stick baking parchment before adding to the tops of cakes.

eileen everest's spiced wine cake

This is my mother's recipe for what is one of the best rich fruit cakes I have ever tasted. It has been in my family for several generations and has now been handed down to me. You will need to prepare the dried fruit three days in advance.

SERVES 14 TO 18

FOR THE FRUIT
175 g/6 oz/1 cup sultanas (golden raisins)
175 g/6 oz/1 cup raisins
100 g/4 oz/³/₄ cup currants
75 g/3 oz/¹/₄ cup glacé (candied) cherries
75 g/3 oz/¹/₂ cup mixed peel
150 ml/5 fl oz/²/₃ cup sherry

FOR THE MARZIPAN
115 g/4 oz/generous ¹/₂ cup caster (superfine) sugar

115 g/4 oz/scant 1 cup icing (confectioner's) sugar, sifted
225 g/8 oz/1¹/₂ cup ground almonds
2 tsps rum or brandy
Few drops of vanilla essence (vanilla extract)
2 egg whites, whisked until foamy

FOR THE CAKE MIX
175 g/6 oz/1¹/₂ sticks butter
175 g/6 oz/generous 1 cup

light muscovado sugar
4 large eggs
100 g/4 oz/1 cup self-raising (self-rising) flour
100 g/4 oz/1 cup plain (all-purpose) flour
Pinch of salt
1 level tsp mixed spice (allspice)
75 g/3 oz/generous ¹/₂ cup ground almonds

225 g/8 oz/1 cup apricot jam (jelly), sieved and warmed

1 Prepare the dried fruit three days ahead. Place the dried fruits into a mixing bowl with the cherries and the mixed peel. Add the sherry and stir until the fruit is well covered. Cover the bowl with plastic wrap and leave for three days, turning the fruit every 24 hours to distribute the sherry juices evenly.

2 Prepare the marzipan the day before baking the cake. Combine the marzipan ingredients with enough egg white to make a soft, moist paste that holds its own shape. Cover with plastic wrap and leave in the fridge to firm up overnight.

3 On the day of baking, beat the butter and sugar in a mixing bowl until light and creamy. Beat in the eggs. Fold in the two types of flour, salt, spice and ground almonds. Drain the fruit and stir it lightly into the cake mixture until well blended. Spoon into a buttered 20-cm (8-in) round cake tin 10-cm (4-in) tall, lined with baking parchment and carefully smooth the top over with a knife.

4 Bake in a preheated oven at 170°C (375°F) for 1 hour. Reduce the temperature to 150°C (300°F) for a further 1¹/₂ hours with the cake loosely covered with double-folded baking parchment to prevent it from over-browning. Remove from the oven and leave the cake in the tin until it is completely cool.

5 Turn out onto a plate and peel off the baking parchment. Brush the cake all over with the warm apricot jam. Divide the marzipan into two equal pieces and reserve one piece, wrapped in a plastic bag, for the decorations.

6 Measure up one side of the cake, across the top and down the other side, then roll out the marzipan onto a sheet of baking parchment until it is a circle whose diameter is slightly larger than this measurement. Invert the whole cake onto the centre of the marzipan and press it gently down so that it sticks evenly over the surface. Turn the cake over and peel away the paper from the marzipan. Smooth over the cake with a rolling pin, carefully working the marzipan into a shape around the edge and sides with the palms of your hands. Use a sharp knife to cut off the excess around the bottom.

7 Carefully slide the cake from your work surface onto your hand, then drop it centrally onto a cake board. Use the reserved piece of marzipan to make fruits, flowers and other decorations and stick them to the top of the cake with a little beaten egg white. Store well wrapped in kitchen paper and a fresh linen napkin in an airtight tin. Stored in this way, the cake will keep for several months.

chocolate pecan and bourbon brownies

This cake is every cook's dream as it can be made about four to five days in advance and will keep moist and fudgy if kept well wrapped in an airtight tin. Serve cut into squares.

MAKES 16 SQUARES

115 g/4 oz 70% cocoa (bittersweet) chocolate, roughly broken
175 g/6 oz dark (semisweet) chocolate, roughly broken
35 g/1¼ oz/¼ cup cocoa

(unsweetened cocoa), sifted
175 g/6 oz/1½ sticks butter
1 tsp vanilla extract
1 tbsp bourbon whiskey, (optional)
5 medium eggs

280 g/10 oz/scant 1½ cups caster (superfine) sugar
115 g/4 oz/1 cup pecans or walnuts

1 Preheat the oven to 190°C (375°F). Melt the two types of chocolate, cocoa, butter and vanilla with the whiskey, if using, in a mixing bowl set over a pan of hot water taken off the heat, stirring occasionally.

2 Place the eggs and sugar in a large mixing bowl and whisk together for 30 seconds. Set the bowl over a pan of simmering water ensuring that the bowl does not touch the water. Using an electric hand whisk, whisk the mixture for about 5 minutes until it looks thick and billowy and leaves a trail. Remove from the heat and whisk for 2 more minutes.

3 Carefully fold the chocolate mixture into the pale, creamy mixture until it starts to look evenly coloured. Gradually add the nuts. Over mixing will knock out some of the air so it might be advisable to add the nuts when the two mixtures are only half combined then to carry on folding the mixture until thoroughly incorporated. Pour into a 23-cm (9-in) square tin 4 cm (1½ in) deep lined at the base with baking parchment and bake for 50 minutes. Freezing is not recommended for this cake.

simnel cake

The top of this ever popular Easter cake is covered with a delicious home-made marzipan which is finished off with caramelized icing sugar. Make sure to soak the fruit in the sherry three days beforehand as it gives the cake a very special flavour and moist crumb.

SERVES 12 TO 16

FOR THE FRUIT
175 g/6 oz/1 cup dried mango, chopped
175 g/6 oz/1 cup sultanas (golden raisins)
115 g/4 oz/³⁄₄ cup mixed candied peel, chopped
150 ml/5 fl oz/²⁄₃ cup sherry

FOR THE MARZIPAN
350 g/12 oz/2¹⁄₂ cups ground almonds
175 g/6 oz/1¹⁄₄ cups icing (confectioner's) sugar
175 g/6 oz/scant 1 cup caster (superfine) sugar
1–2 small egg whites, lightly whisked
1–2 tbsps brandy, (optional)

FOR THE CAKE MIX
175 g/6 oz/1¹⁄₂ sticks butter at room temperature
175 g/6 oz/generous 1 cup light muscovado cane sugar
3 medium eggs
300 g/10¹⁄₂ oz/2¹⁄₂ cups self-raising (self-rising) flour
Pinch of salt
2 tsps mixed spice (allspice)
Rind of 1 large orange, finely grated
Juice of ¹⁄₂ orange
2 tbsps apricot jam (jelly) mixed with 1 tbsp water, heated and strained, for the glaze
Icing (confectioner's) sugar, to dust

1 To prepare the fruit, place the dried fruits into a medium-size mixing bowl with the peel. Add the sherry and stir until they are well covered. Leave to soak up the juices for three days, covered at room temperature.

2 On the day of cooking, prepare the marzipan. Place the almonds and two types of sugar in a food processor and whizz them together into a fine powder. Combine the almond mixture with enough of the whisked egg white and brandy, if using, to make a firm, moist ball of paste. Divide the paste into two balls: one weighing 225 g (8 oz) and the other 450 g (1 lb). Wrap in plastic wrap and refrigerate for 1 to 2 hours until firm. Remove the smaller ball of paste from the fridge. Roll it into a 20-cm (8-in) circle and refrigerate until required.

3 Preheat the oven to 150°C (300°F). Beat the butter and sugar until they are light and creamy. Beat in the eggs gradually, then fold in the flour, salt and spice. Drain the macerated fruit and stir it lightly into the cake mixture with the orange rind and juice.

4 Spoon half the cake mixture into a lightly buttered 20-cm (8-in) round tin 7½ cm (3 in) deep lined at the base and sides with baking parchment and level off the surface with a spatula. Place the circle of marzipan on top, then spoon over the remaining cake mixture and level it off. Bake for 1 hour 45 minutes. When it has cooled, turn it out onto a wire cooling rack and carefully peel away the lining paper. Brush a thin layer of hot apricot glaze over the top and sides of the cake.

5 Meanwhile, remove the larger ball of marzipan from the fridge, setting aside 100 g (3½ oz) for the cake decorations. Roll it into a circle a little larger than the circumference of the cake, then press it centrally on top of the cake. Using scissors cut a zigzag pattern around the edge of the marzipan, then using the forefinger of one hand, press the points between the forefinger and thumb of the other hand to round them off.

6 To caramelize the marzipan topping, add a light dusting of icing sugar over the surface then place the cake briefly under a moderate grill until it turns light golden in parts. To finish, pipe a little thin icing made with 55 g (2 oz) icing sugar and 1½ tablespoons of warm water in a cobweb pattern over the top and decorate with tiny coloured eggs bought from a sweet shop and moulded marzipan hares made with the reserved marzipan from Step 5.

rich chocolate truffle cakes

Melted chocolate can be softened by adding fresh cream and flavourings to make a paste that can be moulded into small balls to make luxurious truffles. These make an exciting filling to these rich chocolate cakes. Buy quality chocolate truffles for this recipe, or make your own if you prefer. You will require wax paper muffin cases.

MAKES ABOUT 10

175 g (6 oz) 70% cocoa (bittersweet) chocolate
150 g/5½ oz/1½ sticks butter
4 large eggs, separated
175 g/6 oz/1¼ cups icing (confectioner's) sugar, sifted

70 g/2½ oz/½ cup ground almonds, sifted
85 g/3 oz/½ cup cornflour (cornstarch), sifted
1 tsp pure vanilla extract

10 chocolate truffles, flavoured with vanilla or rum
Icing (confectioner's) sugar, to dust

1   Preheat the oven to 200°C (400°F). Butter the holes of a muffin tin and arrange the paper cases inside (or place two paper cases one inside the other for extra strength if using a baking sheet).

2   Melt the chocolate and butter together in a mixing bowl over a pan of hot water taken off the heat. When the ingredients have melted, remove the bowl from the pan. Stir in the egg yolks until well combined followed by the icing sugar, almonds, cornflour and vanilla extract.

3   Meanwhile, in a large, clean bowl, beat the egg whites until stiff then fold carefully into the chocolate mixture until evenly combined. Half fill each case with the chocolate mixture, then lightly press a chocolate truffle into the centre. Fill each case almost to the top with the remaining cake mixture and bake for 15 minutes. Lower the heat to 180°C (350°F) and cook for a further 15 to 20 minutes, until the tops of the cakes look rounded and feel slightly springy to the touch. To serve, dust the tops of the cakes with sifted icing sugar, or drizzle with vanilla or chocolate glaze.

vanilla glaze
85 g/3 oz/¾ cup double-sifted icing (confectioner's) sugar
1 tbsp boiling water
¼ tsp pure vanilla extract

chocolate glaze
85 g/3 oz/¾ cup double-sifted icing (confectioner's) sugar
1 tbsp boiling water
¼ tsp pure vanilla extract
55 g (2 oz) dark (semisweet) chocolate, melted

Whether making the vanilla or chocolate glaze, beat all the ingredients together in a small mixing bowl until smooth and drizzle over the cakes while still warm.

coffee éclairs

This basic choux paste can be piped into little round buns as well as finger-shaped éclairs. For the coffee fondant, add a shot of strong coffee to the basic fondant recipe or to double-sifted icing sugar to make a simple icing.

MAKES 12

150 g/5½ oz/1¼ cups plain (all-purpose) flour
1 tsp salt
1 tsp caster (superfine) sugar
100 g/3½ oz/scant 1 stick unsalted (sweet) butter
250 ml (8½ fl oz) water

4 large eggs, lightly beaten
Egg glaze (see page 9)

FOR THE FILLING
Vanilla cream (see page 9), or chestnut cream (see page 117)

FOR THE FONDANT
Half quantity of fondant (see page 10)

1 In a mixing bowl, sift the flour, salt and sugar and set aside. Bring the butter and water just to the boil then remove from the heat. Pour the flour mixture into the water and butter all at once and beat it vigorously with a wooden spatula until the consistency is smooth. Return to the heat for about one minute, beating continuously until the paste is dry and comes away from the sides and bottom of the pan in a ball. Remove from the heat and leave it to cool slightly.

2 Set aside one beaten egg. Using an electric whisk, beat the remaining three beaten eggs a little at a time, into the warm paste, mixing thoroughly between each addition. Beat in enough of the reserved egg (you may not need it all), to make a shiny mixture which should fall from the spoon when sharply shaken (if the mixture is too loose it will spread more freely during baking and will not rise properly).

3 Lightly butter two baking sheets and set them in the fridge to chill. Fill a large piping bag fitted with a large star nozzle and pipe the mixture into 8-cm (3¼-in) lengths at well spaced intervals onto the chilled baking sheets. Lightly brush a small amount of egg glaze along the tops and score lengthways with a fork dipped in egg glaze.

4 Bake in a preheated oven at 200°C (400°F) for about 20 minutes until fully risen and golden. Transfer to cool on a wire cooling rack. Using the point of a knife, pierce a hole at one end of the éclairs and using a ½-cm (¼-in) nozzle, pipe with the filling, then dip the top of each éclair into warm coffee fondant. Remove the excess drips with your finger and leave to set.

dried cranberry marzipan cake

Cranberries have a sharp, refreshing taste and go well with marzipan. Dried cranberries won't seep their red juices into the cake and are every bit as delicious as fresh ones.

SERVES 10

Half quantity of fresh
  marzipan (see page 11)
1 tsp vanilla extract
1 tbsp rum
115 g/4 oz/1 stick butter,
  softened
115 g/4 oz/scant ½ cup
  caster (superfine) sugar

3 large eggs, beaten
140 g/5 oz/scant 1 cup dried
  cranberries, roughly chopped
115 g/4 oz/³⁄₄ cup ground
  almonds
2 tsps orange marmalade
115 g/4 oz/1 cup plain
  (all-purpose) flour, sifted

2 lightly rounded tsps baking
  powder, sifted

FOR THE GLAZE
2 tbsps orange marmalade
2 tbsps caster (superfine)
  sugar
2 tbsps water

1 Preheat the oven to 180°C (350°F). Cream the marzipan, vanilla extract, rum, butter and caster sugar together into a smooth paste. Add the eggs, gradually beating them well into the mixture until well combined, then fold in the remaining ingredients.

2 Spoon the mixture into a 2-lb (3-pt) French-style loaf tin lined at the base with baking parchment and bake for about 1 hour. Cover with a double-folded sheet of baking parchment about 10 minutes before the end of baking to ensure the top of the cake does not over-brown. Leave to cool a little before turning out onto a wire cooling rack.

3 To make the glaze, add all the ingredients to a small saucepan and boil together until the syrup thickens. Brush the hot syrup over the surface of the cake.

little moroccan cakes

Make sure to use all the syrup in the recipe as the little cakes need to be saturated. Enjoy with a soothing glass of hot mint tea.

MAKES 18

FOR THE CAKE MIX
85 g/3 oz/³/₄ stick butter
115 g/4 oz/generous ¹/₂ cup caster (superfine) sugar
2 small eggs, lightly beaten
85 ml/3 fl oz/¹/₂ cup water
250 g/9 oz/2¹/₄ cups fine semolina

85 g/3 oz/³/₄ cup ground almonds
1 tsp baking powder
¹/₂ tsp bicarbonate of soda (baking soda)
115 g/4 oz/1 cup pistachio nuts, skinned and finely chopped

FOR THE SYRUP
450 g/1 lb/2¹/₄ cups granulated sugar
350 ml/12 fl oz/1¹/₂ cups water
Juice of 1 lemon

1 Preheat the oven to 180°C (350°F). Cream the butter with the sugar then beat in the eggs until the mixture looks creamy. Stir in the water. In a separate bowl, mix the semolina, ground almonds, baking powder and bicarbonate of soda together and sift into the batter. Mix lightly and pour into a shallow lightly buttered 20 x 30-cm (8 x 12-in) baking tin lined at the base with baking parchment. Carefully smooth over the surface of the batter with a spatula, then sprinkle the crushed pistachios over the top. Bake for about 25 minutes, until the cake looks a pale golden colour and feels firm to the touch. Leave to cool in the tin.

2 To make the syrup, add all the syrup ingredients to a medium-size saucepan and dissolve over a medium heat. Bring to the boil, then reduce the heat and leave on a moderate rolling boil for 10 minutes. While the cake is still warm from the oven, add spoonfuls of the warm syrup slowly to the cake until the last drop is used. When the cake has cooled, cut it into little diamond or square shapes.

organic chocolate cream cake

This rich chocolate cake with a fairly dense crumb is lightly fragranced with spices and topped generously with a smooth and buttery chocolate icing.

SERVES 8 TO 10

140 g (5 oz) organic dark (semisweet) chocolate
250 ml/9 fl oz/generous 1 cup single (light) organic cream
1 tsp vanilla extract
½ tsp ground cinnamon
½ tsp ground cardamom

seeds taken from 7–8 cardamom pods
225 g/8 oz/1 cup organic caster (superfine) sugar
200 g/7 oz/1¾ sticks organic butter
3 large organic eggs, separated

225 g/8 oz/2 cups plain (all-purpose) organic flour
20 g/¾ oz/¼ cup organic cocoa powder (unsweetened)
2 lightly rounded tsps baking powder

1 Preheat the oven to 180°C (350°F). Melt the chocolate and cream in a small saucepan over a low heat stirring continuously. Remove from the heat then stir in the vanilla and spices and set aside.

2 Cream the sugar and butter together until light and fluffy, then beat in the egg yolks one at a time. Add the egg whites to a dry, clean bowl and whisk them until stiff.

3 Sift the flour, cocoa powder and baking powder together and fold gently into the cake mixture, alternately with the spiced chocolate cream until evenly combined ensuring not to over mix. Gently fold the egg whites into the mixture. Spoon into a lightly buttered 23-cm (9-in) round loose-bottomed tin lined at the base with baking parchment and smooth the top level with the back of a spoon.

4 Bake in the centre of the oven for 50 minutes until the centre of the cake is firm to the touch, but check the cake after 35 minutes and if the top browns too quickly, cover with a double-folded sheet of baking parchment. Leave to cool slightly before turning out onto a wire cooling rack, then ice generously with chocolate buttercream icing.

chocolate buttercream icing

225 g (8 oz) dark (semisweet) chocolate

85 g/3 oz/¾ stick butter
1¼ tbsps strong, black coffee

125 g/4½ oz/scant 1 cup double-sifted icing (confectioner's) sugar

Melt the chocolate, butter and coffee together in a mixing bowl placed over a pan of hot water taken off the heat and set aside to cool a little. Stir in the icing sugar until smooth. Pour onto the centre of the cooled cake and spread thickly over the surface. Leave the icing to cool and firm. Make extra if you wish to split the cake and fill it.

polka dot fairy cakes

These are the perfect tea party cakes. To make them extra pretty, add coloured sugar in pretty shapes through a stencil to the icing on top. A round-shaped stencil, as used here, adds a pretty polka dot pattern to the surface of each cake. Add several different coloured sugar polka dots if you wish. You will require wax paper cake cases.

MAKES 12

FOR THE MIX
2 large eggs
115 g/4 oz/generous ½ cup
  caster (superfine) sugar
50 ml/2 fl oz/¼ cup double
  (heavy) cream
Zest of 1 lemon, grated

115 g/4 oz/1 cup self-raising
  (self-rising) flour
1 tsp baking powder
50 g/1¾ oz/½ stick butter,
  melted

FOR THE ICING
225 g/8 oz/1¾ cups icing
  (confectioner's) sugar,
  double sifted
3–4 tbsps lemon juice

Coloured sugar, to decorate
  (see page 9)

1 Preheat the oven to 180ºC (350°F). Lightly beat the eggs with the sugar. Beat the cream into the egg mixture for about 1 minute, then add the lemon zest. Fold in the flour sifted with the baking powder, then fold in the melted butter.

2 Three-quarters fill the paper cases with the cake mixture. Set the cases on a baking sheet in the centre of the oven and bake for 12 to 15 minutes until well risen and golden. Test by lightly pressing the cakes with your fingers. The sponge should be golden and lightly spring back. Transfer to a wire cooling rack to cool slightly.

3 To make the icing, sift the icing sugar into a mixing bowl and stir in the lemon juice until the consistency is smooth and shiny. Add a slightly rounded teaspoon of the icing over the centre of each fairy cake and coax it lightly with a knife to evenly coat the surface. When the icing has almost set, place a small stencil with a cut out circle over the top and sprinkle over some coloured sugar.

chocolate and marshmallow wedges

Adults and children alike will love this quirky chocolate cake marbled with pink and white marshmallows. Serve it sliced or wrapped in cellophane and ribbons to make an attractive party going-home gift for the kids.

MAKES 8 SLICES

350 g/12 oz dark (semisweet) chocolate
250 g/9 oz/2¼ sticks butter
1½ tbsps water
1½ tbsps caster (superfine) sugar

1½ tsps vanilla extract
1½ tbsps orange juice
3 medium egg yolks, whisked lightly and strained
125 g/4½ oz digestive biscuits (graham crackers)

175 g/6 oz/⅔ cup pink and white marshmallows
1 tbsp cocoa powder mixed with chocolate powder in equal amounts, to dust

1 Melt the chocolate with the butter, water and sugar in a mixing bowl set over a pan of hot water taken off the heat. Stir until smooth, then remove the bowl from the heat and leave the mixture to cool a little.

2 Lightly whisk in the vanilla and orange juice followed by the egg yolks. Finely crush half of the biscuits and mix them into the chocolate mixture, followed by the remaining digestive biscuits roughly chopped. Finally add the marshmallows cut into halves and quarters. While the chocolate marshmallow mixture is still fairly fluid, pour it into a lightly buttered 20-cm (8-in) round tin lined at the base with baking parchment. If the mixture has begun to set, press it into the tin and then smooth the top level with a palette knife. Cover the tin with plastic wrap and refrigerate for six hours, or preferably overnight until hard.

3 Turn out onto a plate and dust over the top of the cake with cocoa powder evenly mixed with chocolate powder. Cut the chocolate marshmallow biscuit cake into thick wedges while it is still chilled. Wrap in cellophane and tie each one with ribbon. Keep refrigerated until required.

perfect victoria sponge cake

This recipe has proved to be a cook's boon as all the ingredients are mixed together in a food processor. Just a few pulses are all that is needed as the secret of this wonderful sponge cake is to under mix it.

SERVES 9

175 g/6 oz/1½ sticks butter at room temperature, softened

175 g/6 oz/scant 1 cup caster (superfine) sugar
175 g/6 oz/1½ cups self-raising (self-rising) flour

3 medium eggs, at room temperature

1 Preheat the oven to 180°C (350°F). Place all the ingredients into the bowl of a food processor. Pulse the button just enough to bring the ingredients together. Remove the lid and scrape down the sides. Press the pulse button 3 or 4 more times, pausing between each, until the cake mix is soft and smooth.

2 Divide the mixture into two lightly buttered 18-cm (7-in) round sandwich tins lined at the base with baking parchment and bake for 22 to 25 minutes. Turn the cakes out onto a wire cooling rack to cool. Fill and cover with any of the fillings and icings on pages 9 and 10.

tarts and tartlets

The word 'pie', it is said, derives from the magpie: just as this bird is a hoarder of sparkly objects, so a pie can conceal an assortment of ingredients, from the simplest sweet fluffy mass of Bramley apples and cloves set under a crackling sugary crust to a toothsome sweet toffee sauce covered with a layer of bananas and a swathe of coffee cream in the unique and decadent Banoffi pie.

Free-form pies are made with scraps of pastry pressed together and wrapped around a fruit filling, without too much fuss or pretension. Then there are the French style open-faced tarts and tartlets, spilling with fresh and colourful berries that sparkle like jewels sealed under jam glazes. Or there is the upside-down apple tart invented by the Tatin sisters, glossy with a sweet syrupy caramel set in a golden puffy case.

With few exceptions, home-made pastry is always more desirable than the shop-bought variety. For the Tatins, commercial ready-rolled frozen puff pastry is suitable because the pastry will soak up all the buttery juices and the quality of the pastry will be barely noticeable. When using frozen puff pastry, always defrost it in the fridge and keep it chilled until needed so that it remains firm and manageable.

individual pear tarte tatin

You will require four lightly buttered 10-cm (4-in) round tart tins or baby cake pans 2.5 cm (1 in) deep. If you prefer, you can add apples instead of pears for these pretty individual tarts.

MAKES 4

70 g/2½ oz/½ stick butter
70 g/2½ oz/⅓ cup demerara (raw brown), or soft light brown sugar

1 tbsp natural yoghurt
450 g (1 lb) ready-rolled frozen puff pastry, defrosted
2 ripe pears, peeled and halved

Icing (confectioner's) sugar, to dust
Cream or crème fraîche, to serve

1 Preheat the oven to 190ºC (375ºF). Heat the butter and sugar gently together in a saucepan over a low heat and stir for about 1 minute until the consistency is thick and syrupy. Stir in the yoghurt and remove from the heat.

2 Roll out the chilled pastry to a ½-cm (¼-in) thickness. Place the base of one the tins onto the rolled out pastry and use it as a guide to cut a circle 1 cm (½ in) larger than the tin. Make three more circles in the same way.

3 Divide the caramel syrup evenly between the four tins. Using a teaspoon, take a small scoop out of each pear half to remove the core and press each half, cut-side down, into the caramel. Lay each circle of pastry on top of the pear, tucking the extra margin of pastry between the fruit and the sides of the tin.

4 Bake for about 17 to 18 minutes until the pastry is risen, crisp and golden. Leave to cool in the tins for 1 minute to allow the juices to settle then invert them onto four warmed plates. Lightly dust the edges of the tarts with icing sugar and serve them hot with chilled pouring cream or crème fraîche.

pear and banana tarte tatin

Pear and banana make a pleasing alternative filling to the classic apple tarte Tatin.

SERVES 4 TO 6

70 g/2½ oz/½ stick butter, softened

70 g/2½ oz/scant ½ cup caster (superfine) sugar

3 bananas, peeled and halved lengthways

3 ripe pears, peeled, halved and cored

1 tbsp eau de vie liqueur, (optional)

225 g/8 oz ready-rolled frozen puff pastry, defrosted

Crème fraîche, to serve

1 Thickly butter the base and sides of a 20-cm (8-in) round tarte Tatin tin 5 cm (2 in) deep, and evenly sprinkle over the sugar. Arrange the bananas and pears, rounded side down, to fit the tin. Drizzle over the liqueur, if using. Cover with a plate that fits neatly inside the tin and cover with kitchen foil to keep in the steam which helps cook the fruit.

2 Cook on the hob for 7 to 8 minutes over a moderate heat. Remove the foil and the plate and cook further until the juices caramelize and look mid-golden. Remove the tin from the hob and set aside to cool slightly.

3 Preheat the oven to 190º C (375ºF). Roll out the chilled pastry on a lightly floured board to a 0.5-cm (¼-in) thickness. Cut from it a circle 1 cm (½-in) larger than the base of the tin. Lay it over the cooled fruit, tucking the extra margin of pastry between the fruit and the sides of the tin. Bake for 20 minutes then leave to cool in the tin for 1 minute to allow the juices to settle.

4 To turn out, loosely slide a knife around the edges of the pastry and the tin. Cover the tin with a large serving plate, turn upside-down and give the tin one firm shake to release the tart. Serve warm, with a dollop of crème fraîche.

49

apple and cinnamon tarte tatin

This classic upside-down tart looks its best when it is freshly turned out from the tart tin. Eat it warm, while the apples look glossy and amber-coloured and the sweet syrupy juices have slightly settled and thickened.

SERVES 4 TO 6

70 g/2¹/₂ oz/¹/₂ stick butter, softened

70 g/2¹/₂ oz/scant ¹/₂ cup caster (superfine) sugar

5 Cox's apples, peeled, halved and cored

2 cinnamon sticks

225 g/8 oz ready-rolled frozen puff pastry, defrosted

Small sprigs of fresh mint leaves, to decorate

Vanilla ice cream or crème fraîche, to serve

1 Thickly butter the base and sides of a 20-cm (8-in) round tarte Tatin tin 5 cm (2 in) deep, and evenly sprinkle over the sugar. Arrange the apples shoulder to shoulder in a neat layer, rounded side down, over the butter and sugar. Press the cinnamon sticks between them. Cover with a plate that fits neatly inside the tin and cover with kitchen foil, sealing it around the edges of the tin.

2 Cook on the hob for 10 minutes over a moderate heat. This will brown the underside of the apples. Remove the foil and the plate. The syrupy juices should look mid-golden. If they still look pale and thin, cook for a few more minutes, uncovered, so that the juices simmer, reduce and caramelize to the right colour. Remove the tin from the hob and set aside to cool slightly.

3 Preheat the oven to 190°C (375°F). Roll out the chilled pastry on a lightly floured board to a ¹/₂ cm (¹/₄ in) thickness. Cut from it a circle 1 cm (¹/₂ in) larger than the base of the tin. Lay it over the cooled apples, tucking the extra margin of pastry between the apples and the sides of the tin. Bake for 20 minutes and leave to cool in the tin for 1 minute to allow the juices to settle.

4 To turn out, loosely slide a knife around the edges of the pastry and the tin. Cover the tin with a large serving plate, turn upside-down and give the tin one firm shake to release the tart. Serve warm, cut into slices decorated with a sprigs of fresh mint leaves and a scoop of vanilla ice cream or crème fraîche.

caramelized rhubarb tart

This sweet, crisp pastry creates a good balance to the slightly acidic flavour of this delicate pink rhubarb.

SERVES 8

One quantity of sweet pastry, chilled (see page 11)

FOR THE FILLING
800 g/1 lb 12 oz trimmed and prepared young rhubarb (see opposite)

284 ml/10 fl oz/1¼ cups soured (sour) cream
2 large eggs
40 g/1½ oz/¼ cup caster (superfine) sugar
A few drops of pure vanilla extract

2 tbsps fresh orange juice
Zest of ½ orange, finely grated

Icing (confectioner's) sugar, to dust
Vanilla cream (see page 9)

1 Preheat the oven to 190°C (375°F). Thinly roll out the chilled sweet pastry and use it to line a lightly buttered 23-cm (9-in) round loose-bottomed fluted tin. Line the pastry case with kitchen paper and fill with baking beans. Bake blind for 15 minutes, then carefully remove the beans and paper. Reduce the heat to 180°C (350°F).

2 Arrange three-quarters of the prepared rhubarb (see opposite) over the base of the pastry case. Beat the soured cream, eggs, sugar, vanilla, juice and zest together and pour the mixture over the rhubarb. Lightly press the remaining pieces of rhubarb into the mixture and bake for about 25 minutes.

3 Serve warm when it is best, or cold lightly dusted with icing sugar. Alternatively, caramelize the tart by dredging the surface with sifted icing sugar and setting under a moderate grill for 1 to 2 minutes, until the icing sugar melts and turns a rich golden colour. Serve in slices with a dollop of vanilla cream.

to prepare the rhubarb

For extra sweetness, reduce the rhubarb cooking juices until thickened. This method, using the same ingredients, is also good for cooking cranberries or plums which, like rhubarb, are acidic and cook readily into a mush.

85 g/3 oz/½ cup caster
  (superfine) sugar
2 tbsps redcurrant jelly

25 g/1 oz/¼ stick butter
2 tbsps water
800 g/1 lb 12 oz rhubarb, cut
  into 4-cm (1½-in) lengths

½ tsp ground cinnamon, or
  5–6 fresh angelica leaves,
  if in season

1 Preheat the oven to 190°C (375°F). Melt the sugar, jelly, butter and water in a small saucepan over a low heat, then set aside.

2 Pack the rhubarb over the base of a shallow baking tin just large enough to hold the fruit in one layer and sprinkle over the cinnamon or press the angelica leaves between the fruit. Pour over the warm, sweet redcurrant juices from the saucepan and bake for about 8 minutes, carefully turning the fruit in the juices once.

simple apple butter clove pie

Nothing beats the sharp flavours of Bramley cooking apples. Melting mouthfuls of sweetened tender slices of apple are cooked with butter to add flavour to this scrumptious single crust pie that makes the perfect finale to a Sunday roast.

SERVES 4

FOR THE PASTRY
225 g/8 oz/2 cups plain (all-purpose) flour
Pinch of salt
140 g/5 oz/1¼ sticks butter, chopped into small cubes
1 medium egg yolk, whisked with 1–2 tbsps water

FOR THE FILLING
1¼ kg/2 lb 7 oz Bramley (tart) cooking apples, peeled, halved and cored
10 cloves, plus extra for decoration
115 g/4 oz/generous ½ cup caster (superfine) sugar

1½ tbsps butter
Egg glaze (see page 9)

Caster (superfine) sugar, for dusting
Cream, to serve

1 To make the pastry, sieve the flour and salt into a large mixing bowl and add the cubed butter. Using your fingertips, rub the mixture quickly and lightly until it resembles fine breadcrumbs. Use a palette knife to blend enough of the egg and water mix into the crumbs until they begin to cling together. Then press them lightly together to form a soft, moist, but not sticky dough. Very lightly knead the dough on a floured board to smooth out any cracks, then wrap it in a piece of kitchen paper and place it in a plastic bag. Chill in the fridge for 25 minutes before using.

2 To make the filling, slice the apples and add them to a medium-size pan with 1 cup of water, the cloves, sugar and butter. Bring to the boil then immediately reduce the heat, leaving the apples on a gentle simmer until they start to soften. Remove the apples, draining the juices back into the pan and set aside to cool. Turn up the heat and reduce the juices until thick and syrupy.

3 Add the apples to a buttered 23-cm (9-in) round pie dish and pour the warm syrup over the fruit. Thinly roll out the chilled pastry and cover the fruit, placing moist strips of dough painted with egg glaze around the rim first. Trim off the excess pastry with a sharp knife, then cut small decorations from the leftover pastry (pastry leaves look good for fruit pies). Stick them over the pie with egg glaze and prod the crust with 3 or 4 cloves. Chill for 10 to 15 minutes to allow the pastry to firm, then paint over with egg glaze.

4 Bake in a preheated oven at 190°C (375°F) for 30 minutes until the surface of the pie is a rich golden colour. Serve in slices, sprinkled with caster sugar and a drizzle of cream.

Vanilla and spice plum tart

Here, red plums are lightly braised in the oven with spices, sugar and vanilla, then covered in pastry before baking. The mascarpone pastry is deliciously tender and well worth trying for other fruit pies.

SERVES 8

Half quantity of mascarpone and soured (sour) cream pastry, chilled (see page 12)

FOR THE FRUIT
750 g/1 lb 7 oz red plums
1 tbsp redcurrant jelly

½ tsp mixed spice (allspice)
½ tsp pure vanilla bean paste, or seeds from ½ split vanilla pod (vanilla bean)
85 g/3 oz/½ cup golden caster (superfine) sugar

Egg glaze (see page 9)
Cream, to serve

1 Preheat the oven to 190°C (375°F). Wash and dry the plums. Cut some into halves and some into quarters in even amounts and remove the stones. Place them in a 25-cm (10-in) round shallow tin. In a mixing bowl, mix the jelly, mixed spice, vanilla and sugar together and spoon over the plums. Braise them in the oven for 10 minutes, basting them once or twice with the syrup. Set aside to cool.

2 Roll out two-thirds of the chilled pastry into a 33-cm (13-in) circle. Using the rolling pin, lower the pastry into a lightly buttered 20-cm (8-in) round loose-bottomed tin 5 cm (2 in) deep and press it into the edges, leaving the remaining pastry draped over the sides of the tin.

3 Fill the pastry case with the cooled plums, arranging some of the halved plums on top. Spoon the red syrupy juices over the plums and fold the pastry up over the filling to partially enclose the fruit. Paint the pastry with the egg glaze and bake for 25 to 30 minutes until the top looks golden and shiny. Dredge with golden caster sugar and leave the pie to cool a little before carefully removing it from the tin. Serve warm, cut into wedges with a side jug of cream.

Seville orange tart

The pastry for this simple tart is spiced with cardamom then baked with a fresh Seville orange curd filling. Prepare the curd and refrigerate it for at least 12 hours before using.

SERVES 6

FOR THE ORANGE CURD
5 tbsps of orange juice from about 3 Seville (bitter) oranges
Rind of 2 Seville (bitter) oranges, finely grated
2 tsps lemon juice

1 level tsp lemon rind, finely grated
115 g/4 oz/1 stick butter
250 g/9 oz/1¼ cups caster (superfine) sugar
4 large egg yolks and 1 whole large egg, lightly beaten and sieved

Half quantity of orange and cardamom pastry, chilled (see page 12)

Icing (confectioner's) sugar, to dust
Crème fraîche, to serve

1 Start by making the curd. Add all the curd ingredients to a small saucepan and stir the mixture constantly over a moderate heat until it reaches the consistency of thick cream. Remove from the heat immediately and pour into a large, clean jam jar and seal with a lid. Leave overnight in the fridge to set and thicken.

2 The following day, make the pastry. Roll it out thinly on a lightly floured board and use it to line a lightly buttered 23-cm (9-in) round loose-bottomed tin. Prick the base with a fork and refrigerate for 30 minutes. Preheat the oven to 190°C (375°F).

3 Line the pastry case with kitchen paper and fill with baking beans. Bake blind for 15 minutes, then carefully remove the beans and paper. Return to the oven for a further 5 minutes then set aside to cool a little. Spread the base of the pastry case with the curd and bake for 8 to 10 minutes, until the edges look mid-golden but not burnt. Cool slightly before turning out and serve warm cut into slices with a dollop of crème fraîche and lightly dust the edges with icing sugar.

french apple tart with calvados and apricot glaze

To prevent the apple slices for the topping from browning, place the whole peeled apples in a bowl of water and lemon until required. Dry them on kitchen paper, core and slice them as you go along.

SERVES 8 TO 10

Half quantity of brisée pastry, chilled (see page 12)

FOR THE FILLING
700 g/1 lb 9 oz Bramley (tart) cooking apples
25 g/1 oz/¼ stick butter
2½ tbsps caster (superfine) sugar, or golden caster (superfine) sugar

3 tbsps apricot jam (jelly)
1½ tbsps Calvados
1 or 2 tsps lemon juice, to taste

FOR THE TOPPING
650 g/1 lb 7 oz Bramley (tart) cooking apples
15 g/½ oz/1 tbsp butter, melted

55 g/2 oz/generous ¼ cup caster (superfine) sugar
2 tbsps icing (confectioner's) sugar, sifted
Apricot glaze (see page 9)

Crème fraîche, lightly sweetened, or Vanilla cream (see page 9), to serve

1 Preheat the oven to 180°C (350°F). Roll out the chilled pastry thinly and use it to line a buttered 23-cm (9-in) round fluted or plain shallow tart tin. Prick the base with a fork, line it with kitchen paper and fill with baking beans. Bake blind for 10 minutes, then carefully remove the beans and paper. Set aside to cool.

2 To make the filling, peel and cut the cooking apples into small pieces. Add them to a medium-size saucepan with the butter and sugar and cook gently over a low heat for 10 to 15 minutes, stirring occasionally. Whip the soft apple mush into a fluffy purée with the jam, Calvados and lemon juice. Spoon the mixture into the cooled pastry case and level off with the back of a spoon.

3 To make the topping, peel, core and slice the apples as thinly as possible, preferably with a mandolin, into crescent-shaped slices. Arrange the slices over the puréed filling starting from the centre. Rounded side out and half overlapping the slices, work in a concentric pattern until you reach the edges of the tart case. Brush the apples with the melted butter, sprinkle over the sugar and bake in the oven for 20 minutes until the apples are tender and lightly golden around the edges.

4 While the tart is still warm, sift the icing sugar evenly over the apples (not the pastry) and set it under a hot grill for 1 to 2 minutes to caramelize the apples. When done, remove the tart from the grill and brush the warm apricot glaze thickly over the apples. Serve warm or cold with vanilla cream or lightly sweetened crème fraîche.

apricot and almond puffs

These latticed puff pastry cases filled with marzipan and apricots are wonderful, especially when served warm with a little pouring cream, or crème fraîche.

MAKES 9

One quantity of puff pastry, chilled (see page 13)
One quantity of marzipan (see page 11)

Icing (confectioner's) sugar, to dust
Egg glaze (see page 9)
9 fresh ripe but firm apricots, stoned and halved

Icing (confectioner's) sugar, sifted, to glaze
Cream, to serve

1 Preheat the oven to 220°C (425°F). Divide the pastry into two equal pieces and return one piece placed in a plastic bag to the fridge. Roll out the remaining piece into a 33 x 33-cm (13 x 13-in) square.

2 Divide the marzipan into nine equal balls and roll each ball in a little icing sugar. Lightly press the balls to form 7-cm (3-in) circles and place them evenly across the surface of the pastry, leaving 2½ cm (1 in) between each disc and and the edges of the pastry. Paint a little egg glaze around each disc, then press two apricot halves, cut-sides down and slightly overlapping, over the centre of the marzipan.

3 Roll out the second piece of chilled pastry into a 33 x 36-cm (13 x 14-in) rectangle. Use a lattice roller pastry cutter to cut slits into the pastry, then gently ease open the slits to open out the lattice pattern. Carefully roll the latticed pastry around a rolling pin and place it over the marzipan and apricot mounds. Press around them with your fingertips to seal the pastry.

4 Use a 9-cm (3½-in) plain biscuit cutter to stamp out 9 pastries, keeping the little mounds of apricot and marzipan in the centre of each circle. Lightly coat the surface of each pastry with egg glaze before transferring to a lightly greased baking tray. Set the tray on a preheated baking sheet to ensure that the base of the pastries cook thoroughly, and bake the pastries for 15 minutes.

5 Transfer the pastries to a wire grilling rack and dredge them with icing sugar so that the surface of the pastries is completely covered. Set them under a hot grill for 1 to 2 minutes, until the surface turns a caramelized golden colour. Serve warm with a little cream.

pumpkin and almond tart

Candied peel, almonds and pine nuts enhance the flavours of this unique tart. Any left-over pumpkin flesh can be frozen for future tarts.

SERVES 10 TO 12

FOR THE FILLING
450 g/1 lb pumpkin flesh
40 g/1½ oz/scant ½ cup pine nuts
55 g/2 oz flaked (slivered) almonds

175 g/6 oz/scant 1 cup golden (superfine) caster sugar
45 g/1½ oz/¼ cup candied orange peel
55 g/2 oz/scant ½ cup ground almonds

2 tsps flour
450 g (1 lb) shop-bought or home-made puff pastry, chilled (see page 13)

Egg glaze (see page 9)

1 Cut the pumpkin, removed of pith and pips, into 2½-cm (1-in) cubes and boil it fairly briskly in water for about 20 minutes, until it is tender. Drain and purée and return it to the saucepan for a further 1 or 2 minutes, stirring frequently until you have a fragrant, thick consistency. Transfer to a mixing bowl to cool.

2 Preheat the oven to 190°C (375°F). Place the pine nuts and flaked almonds onto a baking sheet and roast them lightly until golden then put them in a liquidizer along with the sugar and candied peel. Whiz into a thick smooth paste then stir into the pumpkin, adding the ground almonds and flour, and mash the mixture until it forms a smooth consistency. Cover and refrigerate while you prepare the puff pastry case.

3 Roll out 250 g (9 oz) of the puff pastry into a 30-cm (12-in) circle. Return the remaining piece to the fridge. Dampen a baking sheet with water lightly shaking off the excess and transfer the pastry circle to the sheet. Brush the edges with egg glaze and roll the edges over twice to make a small rim.

4 Spread the pumpkin filling evenly over the pastry and brush the edges once more with egg glaze. Roll out the remaining pastry into a 13 x 30-cm (5 x 12-in) rectangle and, using a sharp knife, cut nine 1-cm (½-in) wide strips the length of the rectangle. Paint the surface of the strips with egg glaze and arrange over the top of the tart in a lattice pattern. Transfer the tart to the fridge for 25 minutes.

5 Preheat the oven to 220°C (425°F) and bake the tart for 35 minutes until the surface of the pastry looks glossy and richly golden. Leave to cool a little, then carefully ease a palette knife between the pastry base and the tin to loosen it, then slide it onto a large plate. Serve hot or warm, sprinkled with a few extra roasted nuts over the top.

little apple tarts

Bramley apples are one of the pastry cook's favourite fruit. Their sharp flavour, which can be sweetened judiciously, has a real affinity with pastry. Fresh apricots, halved and stoned, make a good alternative if you prefer.

MAKES 4

450 g (1 lb) ready-rolled frozen puff pastry, defrosted
Egg glaze (see page 9)
900 g (2 lb) or 4–5 medium Bramley (tart) apples

30 g/1 oz/¼ sticks butter, melted
4 level tbsps caster (superfine) sugar, sifted

Icing (confectioner's) sugar, to dust
Crème fraîche, lightly sweetened, to serve

1 Preheat the oven to 200°C (400°F). Roll out the chilled pastry so that it is large enough to cut four circles of pastry using a tea saucer as a guide to cut around. Evenly space the pastry circles apart onto a large buttered baking sheet and lightly brush around the edges of the circles with egg glaze.

2 Peel, core and slice the apples as thinly as possible and arrange the slices, rounded side out, from the centre of the tart working outwards and half overlapping the slices. Leave a 1-cm (½-in) margin between the edges of the pastry and the apples. Brush the surface of the apples with the melted butter and sprinkle 1 tablespoon of caster sugar evenly over the surface of each tart.

3 Bake for about 15 minutes until the pastry is lightly golden and gently puffed up. Remove from the oven and dredge each tart with icing sugar, avoiding the edges of the pastry. Place the tarts under a hot grill for 1 to 2 minutes until the apples look richly caramelized around the edges. Serve warm with a dollop of crème fraîche lightly sweetened with sugar or honey.

sweet potato and pecan pie

Bourbon cream goes particularly well with this delicious American pie, or try it with
crème fraîche or vanilla ice cream.

SERVES 8 TO 10

FOR THE FILLING
450 g/1 lb sweet potatoes
70 g/2½ oz/½ cup demerara
  (raw brown) sugar
1 small egg, lightly beaten
1 tbsp double (heavy) cream
1 tbsp butter
½ tsp mixed spice (allspice)
Pinch of salt

FOR THE PASTRY
One quantity of sweet pastry,

chilled (see page 11)
Egg glaze (see page 9)

FOR THE SYRUP TOPPING
1 tbsp double (heavy) cream
75 g/2¾ oz/generous ½ cup
  demerara (raw brown) sugar
50 ml/2 fl oz/¼ cup maple
  syrup
2 tbsps unsalted (sweet)
  butter, softened
1½ tsps vanilla extract

2 small eggs, lightly beaten
115 g/4 oz/1 cup pecans

FOR THE BOURBON CREAM
300 ml/10 fl oz/1¼ cups
  double (heavy) cream
1 tbsp icing (confectioner's)
  sugar, sifted
1 tbsp bourbon whiskey

Icing (confectioner's) sugar,
  to decorate

1 To make the sweet potato filling, prick the sweet potatoes with a fork and bake them
in a hot oven at 220ºC (425ºF) for about 1 hour. When the potatoes are soft to the
point of an inserted knife, remove them from the oven and leave them to cool slightly
before peeling them. Add the flesh to a mixing bowl with the sugar, egg, cream,
butter, mixed spice and salt. Mix thoroughly and set aside to cool.

2 Reduce the oven temperature to 190°C (375°F). Roll out the chilled pastry on a lightly floured board and use it to line a buttered 23-cm (9-in) round loose-bottomed fluted tart tin 5 cm (2 in) deep. Refrigerate for 20 minutes. Prick the base with a fork then line the pastry case with kitchen paper and fill with baking beans. Bake blind for 20 minutes then carefully remove the beans and paper. Set aside to cool slightly before brushing the edges with egg glaze. Return to the oven for a further 5 minutes then pile the sweet potato mixture into the pastry case and set aside.

3 To make the maple syrup topping, beat the cream, sugar, maple syrup, butter, vanilla and eggs together, then stir in the pecans. Pour the syrup over the sweet potato filling and bake for 35 minutes until the surface of the pie looks golden and puffed up. Serve warm in slices lightly dusted with icing sugar and serve with dollops of bourbon cream made by whipping the cream into soft peaks then folding in the icing sugar and a shot of bourbon.

goat's cheese tart with candied fruit

This unusual recipe by Paul Gayler, Chef de Cuisine at the Lanesborough Hotel in London, tastes heavenly served slightly warm, and lightly dusted with icing sugar.

SERVES 8 TO 10

One quantity of sweet pastry, chilled (see page 11)
Egg glaze (see page 9)

FOR THE FILLING
4 large eggs
175 g/6 oz/scant 1 cup caster (superfine) sugar

3 tbsps double (heavy) cream
225 g (8 oz) unsalted goat's cheese
4 tbsps candied fruit, glacé (candied) cherries and orange and lemon peel, finely chopped

Zest of 1½ oranges
1½ tbsps pistachios, skinned and chopped

Icing (confectioner's) sugar, to dust

1 Preheat the oven to 190°C (350°F). Roll out the chilled pastry and use it to line a buttered 23-cm (9-in) round loose-bottomed fluted tart tin 5 cm (2 in) deep. Line the pastry case with kitchen paper and fill with baking beans. Bake blind for 10 to 15 minutes, then carefully remove the beans and paper. Brush the edges of the pastry with egg glaze and return to the oven for a further 5 minutes.

2 To make the filling, beat the eggs and sugar together followed by the cream and goat's cheese breaking down the lumps with a whisk or fork until fairly smooth. Mix in the candied fruit, orange zest and pistachios, until evenly distributed into the mixture. Spoon into the pastry case and bake for 40 minutes until the top of the tart is a rich golden brown. Serve warm or cold with a light dusting of icing sugar.

fresh fig and cherry tart

In summer, decorate the tart with twigs of fresh cherry leaves which make a very pretty presentation. In winter, substitute French Agen prunes for cherries and fresh figs and use armagnac instead of kirsch. This recipe can be converted to individual tartlets, when you will need four 10-cm (4-in) loose-bottomed tins. Divide the pastry, filling and glaze between the tins and prepare as below. Cook for about 20 minutes, or until the tartlets look golden and puffed up.

SERVES 10

FOR THE PASTRY
Half quantity of brisée pastry, chilled (see page 12)

FOR THE FILLING
225 g/8 oz/1½ cups plump sweet red cherries, stoned (pitted)
2 fresh purple figs

100 g/3½ oz/scant 1 cup whole almonds or hazelnuts
100 g/3½ oz/¾ stick butter
75 g/3 oz/½ cup caster (superfine) sugar
1 large egg and 1 large egg yolk
2 tsps kirsch
2 level tbsps plain (all-purpose) flour

FOR THE GLAZE
3 tbsps redcurrant jelly
1–2 tbsps clear, runny, lavender honey
1 tbsp kirsch

Crème fraîche or thick cream, to serve

1 Preheat the oven to 190°C (375°F). Roll out the chilled pastry so that it is large enough to line a buttered 25-cm (10-in) round loose-bottomed plain or fluted tin 2½ cm (1 in) deep. Refrigerate for 30 minutes. Line the pastry case with kitchen paper and fill with baking beans. Bake blind for 10 minutes, then carefully remove the beans and paper.

2 To make the filling, lay the stoned cherries over kitchen paper to allow as much of the juice to drain away as possible. Slice each fig into four pieces. Remove the skin from the nuts and grind them in a food processor to a fine powder, then set aside.

3 Cream the butter and sugar, then beat in the eggs gradually. Stir in the ground nuts, kirsch and flour. Spread the mixture over the base of the cooled pastry case, then lightly press the sliced figs and cherries into the mixture and bake for 30 minutes or until the filling puffs up between the fruit.

4 Meanwhile, prepare the glaze. Add the jelly and honey to a small saucepan. Bring to the boil then simmer for 1 minute. Add the kirsch and stir the jelly gently for a further minute to ease out any lumps until it looks smooth and has thickened. While still hot, thinly brush over the surface of the tart to add shine and flavour. Serve warm or cold with dollops of crème fraîche or thick chilled cream.

strawberry and ginger cheesecake tartlets

You can substitute the ginger syrup with orange liqueur or strawberry jam to add extra sweetness and flavour to the curd cheese mixture. You might also try other fruits such as raspberries, orange segments or an arrangement of whole and sliced fruits. For a pretty finish, decorate the top of the tartlets with strawberry leaves dusted with icing sugar.

MAKES 6

One quantity of rich sweet
  pastry, chilled (see page 12)
450 g/1 lb/2 cups fresh curd
  cheese
55 g/2 oz/¼ cup caster
  (superfine) sugar
1½ tbsps ginger syrup
  (from the stem (preserved)
  ginger jar)
2 large egg yolks
½ tsp pure vanilla extract
2 pieces of stem (preserved)
  ginger, finely chopped,
  (optional)
225 g/8 oz/1 cup fresh
  strawberries, sliced
Icing (confectioner's) sugar,
  sifted
Extra ginger syrup

1 Lightly grease six 9-cm (3½-in) round loose-bottomed tartlet tins 3 cm (1¼ in) deep. Roll out the chilled pastry thinly and use it to line the bottom and sides of the tins. Refrigerate for 20 minutes. Meanwhile, put the cheese into a mixing bowl and combine it with the sugar, ginger syrup, egg yolks and vanilla. Refrigerate alongside the tartlets.

2 Preheat the oven to 180°C (350°F). Fill each tartlet tin two-thirds full with the curd cheese mixture and set the tins onto a preheated baking sheet and bake for 20 minutes until the edges of the pastry are a rich golden colour.

3 Set aside to cool, then turn out onto a wire cooling rack. Sprinkle the chopped ginger (if using) over the tartlets and decorate with the strawberries. Lightly dust with icing sugar and drizzle over extra ginger syrup just before serving.

tarte citron

This is a simple and very successful recipe, providing the lemon custard is baked in the oven at a very low temperature to achieve a soft, smooth-textured custard with a perfect set that will hold its shape beautifully when it is cold and cut into slices. Fresh free range eggs and fresh lemons are essential for this recipe.

SERVES 8 TO 9

One quantity of sweet pastry, chilled (see page 11)
8 large free range eggs
315 g/11 oz/1½ cups caster (superfine) sugar

225 ml/8 fl oz/1 cup double (heavy) cream
Juice and finely grated rind of 5 unwaxed lemons

Icing (confectioner's) sugar, to dust
Cream, to serve

1 Remove the pastry from the fridge and knead it lightly until smooth. Roll it out and use it to line a lightly buttered round 22-cm (8½-in) loose-bottomed, fluted or plain tart tin 5 cm (2 in) deep. Prick the base and leave a small margin of excess pastry overlapping the edges to allow for any shrinkage as the pastry rests. Refrigerate for 25 minutes.

2 Preheat the oven to 180°C (350°F). Remove the tin from the fridge and trim off the excess pastry. Line the pastry case with kitchen paper and fill with baking beans. Bake blind for 20 minutes, then carefully remove the beans and the paper. Allow the pastry crust to cool in the tin. Reduce the oven temperature to 150°C (300°F).

3 In a mixing bowl, whisk the eggs and add the sugar. Beat well until the sugar has dissolved and the mixture is smooth and creamy. Pour in the cream followed by the lemon juice and rind and continue to whisk until the mixture looks thick and creamy.

4 Pour the mixture into the pastry case until it falls level with the edge, then set it carefully into the oven. Bake for about 35 minutes until the edges of the filling start to set. Turn the heat down to 110°C (225°F) and continue to cook for a further 30 minutes. Turn off the heat but leave the tart inside as the oven cools for a further 15 to 20 minutes. If the filling begins to separate away from the edges of the pastry, remove it from the oven and leave it to cool at room temperature. Serve in slices, dusted lightly with icing sugar and a dribble of cream.

the original banoffi

This famous sweet concoction of banana, cream and toffee was invented by Chef Ian Dowding in an act of spontaneous creation in the kitchens of The Hungry Monk restaurant in Jevington, Sussex. Enjoy it, but beware, banoffi can be addictive!

SERVES 10

FOR THE TOFFEE FILLING
2 large tins condensed milk
One quantity of sweet pastry,
  chilled (see page 11)

FOR THE TOPPING
300 ml/10½ fl oz/1¼ cups
  double (heavy) cream
2 tsps caster (superfine) sugar
1 tsp instant coffee granules
5–6 medium bananas

1 To prepare the toffee filling, stand the tins of condensed milk pierced twice with a can opener, labels removed, in a large saucepan of hot water, ensuring the tops of the tins are above water level. Boil for about 2½ hours. Keep an eye on the watermark and top up with freshly boiled water if the water starts running low. Then remove the tins from the water and allow to completely cool before opening.

2 Preheat the oven to 190°C (375°F). Remove the chilled pastry from the fridge and knead lightly. Roll it out and use it to line a lightly buttered 25-cm (10-in) round loose-bottomed tart tin. Refrigerate for 20 minutes. Line the pastry case with kitchen paper and fill with baking beans. Bake blind for 15 minutes, then carefully remove the beans and the paper. Bake for a further 10 minutes until the base looks lightly coloured and the edges are a mid-golden. Leave to cool before carefully turning out the pastry case from its tin.

3 Evenly spread the toffee from the tins onto the pastry case. Beat the cream with the caster sugar and coffee granules until it forms soft peaks and set aside. Peel the bananas and cut them lengthways. Arrange them over the top of the toffee, their natural bent shape will fill the round shape of the tin perfectly. Trim the bananas to fill any spaces between the fruit. Use a large spatula to carefully spread the cream over the bananas and sprinkle a few extra coffee granules on top which will attractively fleck the cream with coffee coloured splashes. Eat the pie on the same day if you can as the layers seem to slacken and separate, however, it will taste every bit as delicious the following day.

muffins, madeleines and scones

There is no comparison between freshly home-baked muffins and their commercial counterparts. Whether you bake Sunburst, Electric lemon or melt-in-the mouth Raspberry and fig muffins, the art is not to over mix the cake mixture and to add it in uneven dollops to produce a golden, puffy topping. Quality ingredients make luxurious flavours. Try French butter, seeds from a vanilla pod or pure vanilla bean paste, freshly ground spices and exotic fruits as well as wonderful fruits like raspberries, cherries and damsons.

Madeleines are traditionally baked in an oval mould with a shell-patterned bottom to give a perfect shape to the batter that will expand during baking until pale golden brown on top and slightly darker brown around the edges. Traditional madeleines are made with flour, sugar, ground almonds and a generous amount of butter but you can add lemon zest, orange or rose flower waters and pure vanilla.

There's nothing more indulgent than a classic cream tea with scones, butter, home-made jam and clotted cream. You can easily adapt the basic formula with other ingredients: grated apple and spice, molasses and syrup or, for a modern spicy twist, try cheese with authentic Indian chutney, spiced with cayenne pepper and mustard, all imaginative variations on a simple theme.

raspberry and fig muffins

Purple-coloured figs, with their luscious red flesh, and fresh raspberries nestle in this delicious muffin batter which puffs up around them in a golden dome as it bakes.

MAKES 8 TO 9

FOR THE FRUIT
140 g/5 oz/generous ½ cup
 fresh raspberries
1 tbsp (superfine) caster sugar
3 fresh figs

FOR THE MUFFIN MIX
225 g/8 oz/2 cups plain
 (all-purpose) flour
2 rounded tsps baking powder
Pinch of salt
140 g/5 oz/³/₄ cup white or
 golden caster (superfine)
 sugar
85 g/3 oz/³/₄ stick butter
1 large egg, beaten
284 ml/9½ fl oz/1¼ cups
 cultured buttermilk
Zest of ½ small orange,
 finely grated

1 Start by preparing the fruit. Lay the raspberries out in a single layer over a large plate and sprinkle them with the sugar. Slice the figs into 2½-cm (1-in) pieces and set aside with the raspberries.

2 Preheat the oven to 180°C (350°F). To make the muffin mix, sift the dry ingredients into a large mixing bowl. Slowly melt the butter, remove it from the heat and leave to cool slightly before mixing it with the egg, buttermilk and orange zest. Pour the buttermilk mixture over the dry ingredients and fold in gently until just blended. Do not overwork the mixture.

3 Sprinkle most of the fruit over the surface and stir in the muffin mixture until just blended. Reserve a little of fruit so that you can lightly press it into the surface of the mixture as you spoon it into the muffin paper cases set inside the holes of the tin. Three-quarter fill the cases and bake for 22 to 25 minutes. Remove from the oven and turn them out onto a wire cooling rack when they are cool enough to handle.

sweet potato and cranberry muffins

These pale orange-coloured sweet potato muffins glazed with maple syrup have an unusual delicate sweet flavour and aroma, particularly when they are still warm.

MAKES 10

FOR THE FRUIT
200 g/7 oz/³⁄₄ cup fresh or
  defrosted cranberries
15 g/¹⁄₂ oz/1 tbsp butter
55 g/2 oz/generous ¹⁄₄ cup
  caster (superfine) sugar
1 tbsp freshly squeezed
  orange juice

FOR THE MUFFIN MIX
200 g/7 oz sweet potatoes
Knob (piece) of butter
1 tsp mixed spice (allspice)
¹⁄₂ orange rind, grated
225 g/8 oz/2 cups plain
  (all-purpose) flour
2 tsps baking powder
Pinch salt

85 g/3 oz/¹⁄₂ cup caster
  (superfine) sugar
85 g/3 oz/³⁄₄ stick butter
284 ml/9¹⁄₂ fl oz/1¹⁄₄ cups
  buttermilk
1 large egg, lightly beaten

Maple syrup, to finish

1 Preheat the oven to 180°C (375°F). To prepare the fruit, add the cranberries, butter, sugar and orange juice to a medium-size shallow baking tin and cook for 6 to 7 minutes, basting twice until the juices start to run but the fruit remains whole, then remove from the oven and set aside.

2 To make the muffin mix, peel and slice the sweet potatoes and cook them on a fairly energetic boil until tender. Drain well and mash them with a knob of butter into a smooth purée. Mix in the spice and orange rind and set aside.

3 Sift the dry ingredients into a large mixing bowl. Slowly melt the butter, remove it from the heat and leave to cool slightly before mixing it with the buttermilk and the egg and pour it over the dry ingredients along with the puréed sweet potato mixture. Fold gently together until nearly blended then fold in the braised cranberries. Two-thirds fill the muffin paper cases set inside the holes of the tin and bake for 25 to 30 minutes then transfer to a wire cooling rack and brush generously with the maple syrup. Drizzle with extra syrup before serving.

electric lemon muffins

Add a zing to a morning tea break with the freshly baked aromas of lemon and cardamom, the main ingredients in these delicious muffins which are made extra delicious served with lemon curd and a dollop of crème fraîche.

MAKES 8 TO 9

225 g/8 oz/2 cups plain (all-purpose) flour
2 rounded tsps baking powder
Pinch salt
140 g/5 oz/scant ¾ cup caster (superfine) sugar, or 5 tbsps runny honey
1 large egg, beaten

284 ml/9½ fl oz/1¼ cups natural yoghurt
1 tbsp freshly grated unwaxed lemon rind
85 g/3 oz/¾ stick butter, melted
8 cardamom seeds, crushed to a powder

8 very thin slices of lemon, halved, to decorate

Lemon curd (see page 10) and crème fraîche, to serve

1 Preheat the oven to 180°C (350°F). Sift the flour, baking powder and salt into a large mixing bowl. If you are using honey instead of sugar, mix it in along with the egg, yoghurt and lemon rind. Stir the melted butter into the mixture, add the cardamom powder and fold lightly together until just mixed.

2 Spoon the mixture into the muffin paper cases set inside holes of the tin so that they are two-thirds full. Lightly press a few lemon segments over the top of each muffin and bake them for 25 minutes until springy to the touch. When the muffins have cooled slightly, remove them from the tin to a wire cooling rack. Serve with a little dollop of lemon curd and crème fraîche on the side.

chocolate party muffins

The kids will delight in sticking chocolate drops, colourful jelly beans or other favourite small sweets on top of these delicious, chocolatey bakes. Perfect for parties or to add a cheerful note to a school lunch box.

MAKES 10

FOR THE MUFFIN MIX
225 g/8 oz/2 cups plain
   (all-purpose) flour
2 tsps baking powder
Pinch of salt
140 g/5 oz/scant ¾ cup
   golden caster (superfine)
   sugar

85 g/3 oz/¾ stick butter
140 g/5 oz plain (semisweet)
   chocolate
1 large egg
284 ml/9½ fl oz/1¼ cups
   carton of buttermilk
1 tsp vanilla extract

FOR THE ICING
115 g/4 oz/scant 1 cup icing
   (confectioner's) sugar
1½ tbsps hot water
85 g (3 oz) plain (semisweet)
   or milk chocolate, melted
50–60 chocolate drops or
   small sweets (candy)

1 Preheat the oven to 180°C (350°F). Sift the dry ingredients into a large mixing bowl. Slowly melt the butter, remove it from the heat and set aside. Break the chocolate into small pieces and melt it in a bowl set over a pan of hot water taken off the heat.

2 Whisk the egg, buttermilk, vanilla and melted butter together and pour them over the dry ingredients. Fold the ingredients together, then lightly fold in the melted chocolate until the mixture begins to look evenly coloured, taking care not to over mix. Divide the mixture between the muffin paper cases set inside the holes of the tin, until about two-thirds full. Bake for 22 to 25 minutes until springy to the touch.

3 To make the icing, double sift the icing sugar into a mixing bowl and beat in the hot water followed by the melted chocolate until a soft and shiny consistency is achieved. When the muffins have cooled a little, spread the icing over the tops of the cakes, then press over the sweets while it is still liquid.

reunion muffins

Here we have two different-coloured muffin batters made with soured cream, chocolate and orange zest marbled into the muffin paper cases.

MAKES 10

225 g/8 oz/2 cups plain (all-purpose) flour
2 rounded tsps baking powder
Pinch of salt
140 g/5 oz/scant ³/₄ caster (superfine) sugar

1 large egg
284 ml/9¹/₂ fl oz/1¹/₄ cups soured (sour) cream
85 g/3 oz/³/₄ stick butter, melted
115 g (4 oz) plain (semisweet) chocolate, melted

1 lightly rounded tsp cocoa powder (unsweetened)
40 g/1¹/₂ oz/¹/₄ cup chocolate drops
Grated rind of ¹/₂ small orange, (optional)

1 Preheat the oven to 180°C (350°F). Sift the flour, baking powder and salt into a large mixing bowl and mix in the sugar. In another bowl, beat together the egg, soured cream and the cooled melted butter until well blended. Pour over the dry ingredients and lightly fold until just combined.

2 Divide the mixture into two equal halves and mix the melted chocolate, cocoa powder and chocolate drops into one half, and the orange rind, if using, in the other half. Spoon the chocolate and orange mixtures in small alternate blobs into the muffin paper cases set inside the holes of the tin until a little more than two-thirds full. Bake for 20 to 25 minutes, but check after 20 minutes as the chocolate mixture will tend to burn more quickly than the orange one. Cover with a sheet of baking parchment if necessary.

nut butter muffins with peanut butter icing

This is a muffin recipe for those who love the rich nutty flavour of peanut butter and the smoky flavour of maple syrup. Serve the muffins, lightly warmed, at breakfast, spread with extra peanut butter, or add peanut butter icing for a sweet treat at tea time.

MAKES 10 MUFFINS

FOR THE MUFFIN MIX
225 g/8 oz/2 cups plain
  (all-purpose) flour
2 rounded tsps baking powder
70 g/2½ oz/½ cup golden
  caster (superfine) sugar
85 g/3 oz/¾ stick butter
175 g/6 oz/⅔ cup crunchy
  peanut butter

200 ml/7 fl oz/scant 1 cup
  plain yogurt
100 ml/3½ fl oz/½ cup
  Canadian maple syrup
1 large egg, lightly beaten
55 g/2 oz/½ cup cashew nuts,
  halved

FOR THE PEANUT BUTTER ICING
3 tbsps crunchy peanut butter
6 tbsps icing (confectioner's)
  sugar, double sifted
5–6 tbsps hot water

1 Preheat the oven to 180°C (350°F). Sift the flour, baking powder and sugar into a large mixing bowl and set aside. Melt the butter, remove it from the heat and mix in the peanut butter. Mash it lightly with a fork until just softened, then mix in the yoghurt, maple syrup and beaten egg.

2 Pour the yoghurt mix over the dry ingredients. Fold lightly together until just blended, being careful not to over mix. Divide the mixture equally between the muffin paper cases set inside the holes of the tin. Sprinkle some of the cashew nut halves over the centre of each muffin.

3 Bake for about 20 to 25 minutes, but check after 20 minutes. If the cakes feel springy to the touch and look nicely risen and golden they are ready. Transfer them to a wire cooling rack.

4 To make the icing, lightly warm the peanut butter in a small saucepan and remove it from the heat. Mix with the icing sugar and hot water until smooth. Using a teaspoon, coat the tops of the muffins with the warm icing and leave them to set.

sunburst muffins with an orange glaze

These luscious muffins are ideal as an afternoon snack with a frothy cappuccino.
The slightly sour orange glaze perfectly complements the sweetness of these deliciously
light and tasty muffins.

MAKES 9 TO 10

FOR THE MUFFIN MIX
225 g/8 oz/2 cups plain
  (all-purpose) flour
2 rounded tsps baking powder
Pinch of salt
140 g/5 oz/³/₄ cup golden
  caster (superfine) sugar

85 g/3 oz/³/₄ stick butter
1 large egg, lightly beaten
175 ml/6 fl oz/²/₃ cup cultured
  buttermilk
Juice of 1¹/₂ oranges
Zest of 2 oranges, grated
1 tbsp of orange marmalade

FOR THE ORANGE GLAZE
Juice and finely grated zest
  of ¹/₂ orange
5–6 tbsps icing
  (confectioner's) sugar,
  double sifted
1 tsp of marmalade

1   Preheat the oven to 180°C (350°F). To make the muffin mix, sift the dry ingredients
    into a large mixing bowl and set aside. Melt the butter in a small saucepan over a low
    heat, then leave it to cool slightly. In another mixing bowl mix together the egg,
    buttermilk, orange juice and zest, and when cooled, the melted butter.

2   Pour in the buttermilk mixture over the dry ingredients and fold it in gently with
    the marmalade until just blended, making sure not to over mix.

3   Spoon the mixture into muffin paper cases set inside the holes of the tin, almost to
    the top. Bake for 25 minutes until the muffins look golden and puffed up and the
    centres bounce back when lightly touched. Remove from the oven and turn them
    out onto a wire cooling rack.

4   To make the orange glaze, add the orange juice to a small mixing bowl and slowly
    beat in the zest, icing sugar and marmalade. The icing should cover the back of the
    spoon, but still be thin and fluid. Drizzle the icing in a loose zigzag pattern over the
    tops of the muffins about 10 minutes before serving so that the glaze looks fresh
    and shiny.

espresso and maple syrup muffins

You will require a freshly made brew of espresso, or use your own favourite coffee made triple strength for this recipe.

MAKES 8 TO 9

250 g/9 oz/2¼ cups plain (all-purpose) flour
2 rounded tsps baking powder
Pinch of salt
Pinch of cinnamon

55 g/2 oz/¼ cup golden caster (superfine) sugar
1 large egg
85 g/3 oz/¾ stick butter, melted

100 ml/3 fl oz/½ cup maple syrup
100 ml/3 fl oz/½ cup strong espresso coffee
3 tbsps buttermilk
Extra maple syrup, to serve

1 Preheat the oven to 180°C (350°F). Sift the flour, baking powder, salt, cinnamon and sugar into a large mixing bowl.

2 Beat the egg and stir it into the cooled melted butter followed by the maple syrup, coffee and buttermilk. Pour the mixture over the dry ingredients. Fold lightly together until just combined, then spoon the mixture into muffin paper cases set inside the holes of the tin. Bake for about 25 minutes. When the muffins have cooled slightly, remove them from the tin to a wire cooling rack. Serve with extra maple syrup drizzled over the top.

vanilla-scented pear and pecan muffins

You will require five to six large 10-cm (4-in) individual muffin tins 4 cm (1½ in) deep greased with melted butter. You could use the standard muffin tins and peel and cut the pears into small wedges.

MAKES 6 TO 7 LARGE AND 10 TO 11 STANDARD MUFFINS

FOR THE FRUIT
3–4 small ripe pears
40 g/1½ oz/½ stick butter
1 lightly rounded tbsp sugar
3 tbsps water

FOR THE MUFFIN MIX
225 g/8 oz/2 cups plain (all-purpose) flour

2 rounded tsps baking powder
Pinch of salt
2 tsps mixed spice (allspice), or 1 tsp powdered cinnamon, and 1 tsp powdered ginger
140 g/5 oz/¾ cup golden caster (superfine) sugar
1 large egg, lightly beaten

1 tsp lemon zest, finely grated
85 g/3 oz/¾ stick butter, melted
284 ml/9½ fl oz/1¼ cups soured (sour) cream
20 pecan nuts, lightly crushed
Pear leaves and icing (confectioner's) sugar, to decorate

1   Preheat the oven to 180°C (350°F). To prepare the fruit, carefully peel, core and cut the pears into halves lengthways, leaving on the short stems wherever possible. Place the butter, sugar and water into a small frying pan over a low to moderate heat, then sauté the pear halves gently for 6 to 7 minutes until tender. Set aside to cool.

2   Sift the dry ingredients into a large mixing bowl. In a separate bowl, stir the egg, lemon zest, warm melted butter and the soured cream together then gently fold the mixture into the dry ingredients with the pecans until just blended. Add a small dollop of the muffin batter to each tin and press one pear half in each one standing it upright in the batter, then half fill the tins with the remaining muffin batter (half the pear length and its short stem should still be visible). Bake for 25 minutes. To serve, add one or two fresh pear leaves lightly dusted with icing sugar to each muffin to complete the picture.

plain madeleines

Flavourings can be varied at whim: lemon or orange zest, chocolate or vanilla. You will require a large madeleine tin or you can use tiny brioche tins or very small antique patty tins which are sometimes embellished with pretty flower- or shell-patterned motifs.

MAKES 24

115 g/4 oz/½ cup caster (superfine) sugar
115 g/4 oz/1 cup self-raising (self-rising) flour, sifted
Pinch of salt

115 g/4 oz/1 stick butter
3 large eggs
55 g/2 oz/scant ½ cup ground almonds

1 tsp pure vanilla extract, or the seeds from 1 vanilla pod (vanilla bean), or 1½ tsps pure vanilla bean paste
Icing (confectioner's) sugar, to dust, (optional)

1 Mix the sugar, flour and salt together in a mixing bowl. Melt the butter and leave to cool. Lightly beat the eggs and mix them into the dry ingredients. Gradually add the cooled melted butter, ground almonds and vanilla. Mix well but not too vigorously. Cover and refrigerate for 30 minutes to 1 hour.

2 Preheat the oven to 200°C (400°F). Melt a little extra butter and lightly brush it over the madeleine moulds then fill them three-quarters full with the cake mixture. Bake for 9 to10 minutes, or until the cakes look a pale golden colour, are well risen and slightly darker brown around the edges (but not burnt). You may need to cook them in several batches. If so, keep the remaining cake mixture covered until required. Serve the cakes warm with a fine dusting of icing sugar or leave plain.

pistachio madeleines

For a touch of Eastern exotica, use pistachios and orange flower water to delicately enhance the flavour of the madeleines. Pistachio skin is slightly bitter and can be removed by blanching the pistachios for a few seconds in boiling water then rubbing the nuts between a clean tea cloth while still warm.

MAKES 24

70 g/2½ oz/generous ½ cup skinned pistachios
115 g/4 oz/generous ½ cup caster (superfine) sugar

115 g/4 oz/1 cup self-raising (self-rising) flour
Pinch of salt
115 g/4 oz/1 stick butter

3 large eggs
2 tsps orange flower water

1   Grind the nuts finely in a food processor. Transfer them to a mixing bowl and mix in the sugar, sifted flour and salt.

2   Melt the butter and leave to cool. Lightly beat the eggs and mix them into the dry ingredients. Gradually add the cooled melted butter and orange flower water, mixing well but not too vigorously. Cover and refrigerate for 30 minutes to 1 hour.

3   Preheat the oven to 200°C (400°F). Melt a little extra butter and lightly brush it over the madeleine moulds then fill them three-quarters full with the cake mixture. Bake for 9 to 10 minutes, or until the cakes look a pale golden colour, are well risen and slightly darker brown around the edges (but not burnt). You may need to cook them in several batches. If so, keep the remaining cake mixture covered until required. Serve the cakes warm.

fondant-dipped madeleines

In this recipe, delicate pink-coloured madeleines are dipped in melted fondant very lightly tinted with a touch of raspberry juice or food colouring.

MAKES 24 CAKES

100 g/3½ oz/generous ½ cup caster (superfine) sugar
115 g/4 oz/1 cup self-raising (self-rising) flour
Pinch of salt
115 g/4 oz/1 stick butter

3 large eggs
55 g/2 oz/scant ½ cup ground almonds
2 tsps rose water
1 drop of red food colouring, (optional)

Half quantity of fondant, melted (see page 10)
A few drops of fresh raspberry juice, or enough to colour the fondant a pale pink

1   Mix the sugar, sifted flour and salt together in a bowl. Melt the butter and leave to cool. Lightly beat the eggs and mix them into the dry ingredients. Gradually add the cooled butter, ground almonds and rose water. Add the food colouring if using. Mix well but not too vigorously. Cover and refrigerate for 30 minutes to 1 hour.

2   Preheat the oven to 200°C (400°F). Melt a little extra butter and lightly brush it over the madeleine moulds then fill them three-quarters full with the cake mixture. Bake for 9 to 10 minutes, or until the cakes look a pale golden colour, are well risen and slightly darker brown around the edges (but not burnt).

3   Add a few drops of fresh raspberry juice made by pressing several fruits through a fine small sieve to the fondant and half-dip the madeleines. You could also use a drop of red food colouring instead, but take care as a tiny speck of it goes a long way.

chocolate and calvados madeleines

Calvados gives extra flavour to these chocolate-flavoured madeleines. Indulge further and serve them with a creamy cup of hot chocolate.

MAKES 24

55 g/2 oz plain (semisweet) chocolate
100 g/3½ oz/generous ½ cup caster (superfine) sugar
115 g/4 oz/1 cup self-raising (self-rising) flour

Pinch of salt
115 g/4 oz/1 stick butter
3 large eggs
55 g/2 oz/scant ½ cup ground almonds
1 tsp pure vanilla extract, or

1 vanilla pod (vanilla bean), split, or 1½ tsps pure vanilla bean paste
1 tbsp Calvados, (optional)
Icing (confectioner's) sugar, to dust, (optional)

1 Break the chocolate into small pieces and melt it in a bowl set over a pan of hot water taken off the heat. Mix the sugar, sifted flour and salt together in a bowl and set aside. Melt the butter and leave to cool. Lightly beat the eggs and mix them into the dry ingredients. Gradually add the cooled butter, ground almonds and vanilla, followed by the chocolate and Calvados, if using. Stir until the mixture looks evenly coloured with the chocolate, then cover and refrigerate for 30 minutes to 1 hour.

2 Preheat the oven to 200°C (400°F). Melt a little extra butter and lightly it brush over the madeleine moulds then fill them three-quarters full with the cake mixture. Bake for 9 to 10 minutes, or until the cakes are well risen. You may need to cook them in several batches. If so, keep the remaining cake mixture covered until required. Serve the cakes warm with a fine dusting of icing sugar or leave plain.

honey and plum madeleines

Make sure to cut the plums finely so as to keep the pretty moulded shell shaped pattern of the cakes intact. Victoria plums go especially well in this recipe.

MAKES 24

115 g/4 oz/1 cup self-raising (self-rising) flour
Pinch of salt
85 g/3 oz/1/2 cup golden caster (superfine) sugar
3 large eggs, lightly beaten

1 tbsp clear, runny honey
115 g/4 oz/1 stick butter
55 g/2 oz/scant 1/2 cup ground hazelnuts
1 tsp vanilla extract, or the tiny black seeds from 1 vanilla pod (vanilla bean)

6 ripe but firm plums, stoned (pitted) and chopped into very small pieces
Icing (confectioner's) sugar, to dust

1 Sift the flour and salt into a mixing bowl and mix in the sugar. Lightly beat the eggs and honey together and pour over the dry ingredients, mixing until combined. Melt the butter and leave to cool. Gradually add the cooled melted butter, ground hazelnuts and vanilla. Mix lightly together with a large spoon until evenly combined. Cover and refrigerate for 30 minutes to 1 hour.

2 Preheat the oven to 200°C (400°F). Melt a little extra butter and lightly brush it over the madeleine moulds then fill them three-quarters full with the cake mixture. Lightly dot the mixture with pieces of chopped plum. Bake for 9 to10 minutes, or until the cakes look a pale golden colour, are well risen and slightly darker brown around the edges (but not burnt). You may need to cook them in several batches. If so, keep the remaining cake mixture covered until required. Turn out while they are still hot onto a wire cooling rack and dust with a little icing sugar to serve.

drop scones

Here, spoonfuls of scone batter are cooked on a flat griddle to make small, flat-shaped scones similar to pancakes. I find these delicious scones freeze reasonably well. To defrost, leave them at room temperature and warm them very lightly for five to ten minutes under foil in a low oven.

MAKES 10

3 heaped tbsps self-raising (self-rising) flour
1 lightly rounded tbsp caster (superfine) sugar

¼ tsp cream of tartar
1 egg, lightly beaten
4 tbsps milk

Butter, for frying
Butter, jam and thick cream, to serve

1   Sift together the flour, sugar and cream of tartar. Make a well in the centre and drop in the egg with the milk and beat together to make a fairly thick batter with a dropping consistency.

2   Heat a griddle or frying pan and grease it lightly with butter, which should be hot and sizzling before you add the batter. Pour a dessertspoon onto the griddle or pan and when small bubbles start to rise to the surface, turn the scone over with a palette knife and cook it on the other side. Fit as many scones as you can onto the frying pan but make sure you leave enough space between them. When both sides are cooked and golden transfer the scones to a wire cooling rack and serve warm or cold thickly spread with butter, jam and a dollop of thick cream.

apple scones

These apple-scented scones are delicious served warm or cold spread with butter. When quince are in season, they make an unusual substitute for apples, very finely grated.

MAKES 15

225 g/8 oz/2 cups self-raising (self-rising) flour
Pinch of salt
55 g/2 oz/½ stick butter, roughly chopped

55 g/2 oz/generous ¼ cup caster (superfine) sugar
225 g/8 oz Bramley (tart) cooking apple, peeled and grated

70 ml/2½ fl oz/generous ¼ cup milk
Egg glaze (see page 9)

1 Preheat the oven to 200ºC (400ºF). Put the flour, salt and butter into a large mixing bowl and rub in the butter using your fingertips until it resembles fine breadcrumbs. Mix in the sugar and the grated apple and combine with enough of the milk to make a soft dough.

2 Turn onto a floured board and knead lightly. Roll out the dough to a 1–2-cm (½–¾-in) thickness. Then cut into circles with a 5-cm (2-in) floured biscuit cutter. Place the circles onto an ungreased baking sheet, brush over with a little egg glaze and bake for about 10 to 15 minutes. Check the scones after 10 minutes to see how they are progressing. If they looked well risen with golden tops they are ready.

scones à l'indienne

Authentic Indian chutney enhances this simple cheese scone recipe, flavoured with a warm hint of spice. Serve them warm when they are excellent mid-morning with a cup of coffee, or in the afternoon to add a savoury balance to an over-sweet tea.

MAKES 11 TO 12

225 g/8 oz/2 cups plain (all-purpose) flour
Pinch of salt
40 g/1½ oz/½ stick butter

85 g/3 oz mature Cheddar cheese, grated
1 level tsp English mustard powder

½ level tsp cayenne pepper
160 ml/5 fl oz/⅔ cup milk
2 tbsps Indian mango chutney
Egg glaze (see page 9)

1 Preheat the oven to 200ºC (400ºF). In a mixing bowl, sift the flour and salt together. Rub in the butter using your fingertips and lightly mix in the grated cheese, then add the mustard and cayenne pepper. Pour in the milk to make a smooth, fairly firm dough.

2 Knead lightly on a floured board and divide the dough into two equal pieces. Lightly roll each piece out to a 1-cm (½-in) thickness and spread the chutney over one piece of the dough and firmly press the remaining piece on top. Lightly wash with egg glaze and refrigerate for 20 minutes.

3 Lightly roll the dough slab to make it level, then cut it into circles using a 5-cm (2-in) floured plain biscuit cutter. Place them onto a lightly buttered baking sheet and bake for 10 to 12 minutes. Serve warm from the oven. To reheat, wrap the scones in kitchen foil and place in a low preheated oven at 140ºC (275ºF) for about 15 to 20 minutes.

buttermilk scones

Buttermilk scones have a pale yellow colour and a slight acidic tang that contrasts deliciously when they are spread with sweet conserves. Baking powder makes them rise double the size of plain English scones.

MAKES 10 SCONES

225 g/8 oz/2 cups self-raising (self-rising) flour
½ tsp salt
1 level tsp baking powder

40 g/1½ oz/½ stick butter
1 level tbsp caster sugar
140 ml/5 fl oz/⅔ cup buttermilk

Egg glaze (see page 9)
Clotted cream and raspberry or strawberry jam (jelly), to serve

1   Preheat the oven to 200°C (400°F). Sift the flour, salt and baking powder into a large mixing bowl. Rub in the butter using your fingertips and when it resembles fine breadcrumbs, add the sugar and mix to a soft dough with the buttermilk. Turn the dough onto a floured board, and knead lightly. Roll into a 2-cm (¾-in) thick slab then cut into 5-cm (2-in) circles with a floured biscuit cutter.

2   Carefully transfer to a large ungreased baking sheet. Brush the tops with egg glaze and bake for 10 to 15 minutes until lightly golden. Remove from the oven and leave to cool on a wire cooling rack. Serve warm with fresh clotted cream and raspberry, cherry or strawberry jam.

TIP
As with all scones, you can lightly reheat them set on a plate under a loose dome of kitchen foil, sealed around the edges, in a low oven at about 140°C (275°F) for 5 to 10 minutes.

plain english scones

These traditional English scones can be frozen. They defrost in seconds in a microwave and are delicious served with jam and clotted cream. Ideal washed down with a cup of Earl grey or your favourite brew.

MAKES 10

225 g/8 oz/2 cups self-raising (self-rising) flour
½ tsp salt

40 g/1½ oz/½ stick butter
140 ml/5 fl oz/⅔ cup milk
Egg glaze (see page 9)

Clotted cream and raspberry, cherry or strawberry jam (jelly), to serve

1 Preheat the oven to 200°C (400°F). Sift the flour and salt into a mixing bowl. Rub in the butter using your fingertips and when it resembles fine breadcrumbs pour in the milk and mix to a soft dough. Turn the dough onto a floured board and knead lightly. Roll into a 2-cm (¾-in) thick slab and cut into circles with a 5-cm (2-in) floured plain biscuit cutter.

2 Carefully transfer to a large, ungreased baking sheet. Brush the tops with egg glaze and bake for 10 to 15 minutes until lightly golden. Remove from the oven and leave to cool on a wire cooling rack. Serve warm with fresh clotted cream and raspberry, cherry or strawberry jam.

american cornmeal scones

This recipe is a variation on a recipe from one of America's best-known cooks, Martha Stewart. A mixture of flour and cornmeal are used to create a deliciously light crumbly-textured scone – or biscuit as they are known in the States. You can buy cornmeal or ground maize from health food stores.

MAKES 15

225 g/8 oz/2 cups self-raising (self-rising) flour
125 g/4 oz/¾ cup fine, yellow cornmeal
2 lightly rounded tsps baking powder

¾ tsp bicarbonate of soda (baking soda)
½ tsp salt
1½ level tbsps caster (superfine) sugar
175 g/6 oz/1½ sticks butter, cubed

160–175 ml/5–6 fl oz/ ⅔–¾ cup buttermilk
Butter, home-made jams (jellies) or honey, to serve

1 Preheat the oven to 200°C (400°F). Sift all the dry ingredients into a large mixing bowl and mix in the cubed butter. Using your fingertips, lightly rub the ingredients together until the mixture resembles small flakes. Using a large wooden spoon, stir in the buttermilk. You will need enough to make a smooth, moist paste that holds its own shape.

2 Lightly roll out the paste onto a floured board into a 2-cm (¾-in) thick slab, then using a floured 5-cm (2-in) plain biscuit cutter, stamp out 15 scones. Place them on a lightly buttered baking sheet, and bake for 12 to 15 minutes until they look well risen and lightly golden. Serve warm with butter, home-made jams or honey.

molasses scones

These scones are ideal for a quick breakfast or a mid-morning break spread with butter and mashed bananas. For a slightly sweeter flavour and golden colour, substitute golden syrup for treacle in the scone mixture. You can also add 25 g (1 oz) golden sultanas or whatever your preference.

MAKES 10

225 g/8 oz/2 cups self-raising (self-rising) flour	25 g/1 oz/scant ¼ cup caster (superfine) sugar	1 tbsp treacle (dark molasses)
Pinch of salt	40 g/1½ oz/½ stick butter	160 ml/5 fl oz/⅔ cup milk

1 Preheat the oven to 200°C (400°F). Sift the dry ingredients into a large mixing bowl and mix in the butter using your fingertips until the mixture resembles fine breadcrumbs. Make a well in the centre and pour in the treacle then gradually pour the milk over the treacle and stir until evenly mixed then draw in the flour and butter mixture until well combined.

2 Form the mixture into a soft dough and knead it briefly on a lightly floured work surface pushing the dough away from you with the heel of your hand and drawing it back several times until evenly coloured. Do not overwork the dough or the scones will be hard and heavy.

3 Roll the dough out into a 2-cm (¾-in) thick slab. Cut into circles with a plain 5-cm (2-in) floured biscuit cutter and bake on a lightly buttered baking sheet for 10 minutes. Remove from the oven and leave to cool on a wire cooling rack.

loaf cakes and roulades

Loaf cakes is the slightly confusing name given to cakes that are made in tins designed for bread making. The tins can vary from the old-fashioned bread tin to the chic, polished French loaf tin, which is longer and slimmer in shape and designed for any number of culinary purposes, from cakes and breads to savoury pâtés. The recipes for loaf tins use a selection of sizes as well as individual baby loaf tins, but I strongly recommend you choose non-stick ones for these. I often prefer the French version because its slimmer dimensions allow cake mixtures to cook more efficiently.

A roulade is an elegant concoction with a rich mousse-like sponge wrapped in a spiral around a number of decadent, cream-based fillings. The texture of the sponge is made light by adding beaten egg whites folded into the cake mixture and baked for a very short time. It has a tendency to form cracks as it is rolled, which add to its appeal as it looks extremely attractive when dusted with icing sugar.

reunion loaf cake

This attractive union of chocolate and vanilla cake mixtures looks as impressive as it tastes. Do try it.

SERVES 10 TO 12

225 g/8 oz/2 cups self-raising (self-rising) flour
Pinch of salt
1 tsp baking powder
115 g/4 oz/1 stick butter, softened

150 g/5½ oz/scant ¾ cup caster (superfine) sugar
2 large eggs
175 g (6 oz) plain (semisweet) chocolate
¼ tsp coffee granules

dissolved in 1 tsp hot water
125 ml/4 fl oz/½ cup single (light) cream
3½ tbsps soured (sour) cream
1 tsp pure vanilla bean paste or vanilla extract

1 In a large mixing bowl, sift the flour, salt and baking powder and set aside. In a separate bowl, beat the butter and sugar together until creamy. Add the eggs one at a time and mix until light and fluffy.

2 Break the chocolate into small pieces and melt it in a mixing bowl over a pan of hot water taken off the heat. Mix in the coffee and 60 ml (2 fl oz) of the cream and set aside. In a separate bowl, mix the remaining cream with the soured cream. Gradually fold the flour and the soured cream mixture alternately in small amounts at a time into the egg mixture until fully combined.

3 Preheat the oven to 170°C (325°F). Halve the cake mixture and lightly stir one half of it into the warm chocolate cream until evenly coloured, then add the vanilla flavouring to the other half. Lightly butter and line a loose-sided 2-lb (3-pt) French loaf tin. Layer the vanilla and chocolate cake mixtures in rounded tablespoonfuls in alternating colours into the tin keeping in mind you are trying to create a marbled effect.

4 Bake for 50 minutes, but check after 35 to 40 minutes. It is advisable to cover the top loosely with a piece of baking parchment if the top is slightly over-browning. Leave to cool slightly, before releasing the sides of the tin. Lift the cake carefully on to a wire cooling rack. Serve cold cut into slices.

honey spice bread

This sweet bread is delicious spread thickly with butter for breakfast, tea or a morning coffee break. Use fresh spices if you can for the best flavours.

SERVES 10

115 g/4 oz/1 cup shelled nuts to include hazelnuts, walnuts and pine nuts, coarsely chopped	2 tsps baking powder	½ tsp ground cloves
	315 g/11 oz/1½ cups clear, runny honey	2 tsp mixed spice (allspice)
	2 large eggs, lightly beaten	Zest of ½ lemon, finely grated
315 g/11 oz/2¾ cup plain (all-purpose) flour	1 tsp ground ginger	2 tsps baking powder
	½ tsp ground cinnamon	Apricot glaze (see page 9)

1 Preheat the oven to 160°C (325°F). Using a large mixing spoon, lightly mix all the ingredients together in a large mixing bowl until well combined. If the honey is too thick, first warm it lightly until it liquifies. Transfer the mixture to a buttered 2-lb/3-pt/7½-cup loaf tin lined at the base with baking parchment.

2 Bake for about 1 hour until the top looks well risen and firm to the touch. Warm the glaze and thickly brush it over the surface of the warm cake. Serve cold in slices.

organic banana, blueberry and orange loaf cake

Eat it as it comes or set a few slices under a hot grill until the edges look crisp and golden. Spread lightly with butter and enjoy with a glass of fresh organic breakfast milk.

SERVES 10

85 g/3 oz/³⁄₄ stick organic butter, softened
115 g/4 oz/¹⁄₂ cup organic caster (superfine) sugar
1 large organic egg, lightly beaten
225 g/8 oz/2 cups organic self-raising (self-rising) flour

Pinch of salt
2 rounded tsps baking powder
5 organic, medium-size ripe bananas
125 g/4 oz/¹⁄₂ cup organic blueberries
Rind of 2 medium-size organic oranges, finely grated

Rind of 1 unwaxed lemon, finely grated
Icing (confectioner's) sugar, to dust

1 Preheat the oven to 180°C (350°F). Beat the softened butter and sugar together until light and creamy. Gradually add the egg and beat it into the butter and sugar mixture until smooth and well combined.

2 Sift the flour, salt and baking powder into a mixing bowl and set aside. In a separate bowl, mash four of the bananas (reserving one for decoration). Divide the banana mash into two equal portions and add half of it to the creamed butter mixture along with the blueberries and the orange and lemon rinds. Gradually fold in the flour with the remaining mashed bananas until well amalgamated but not over mixed.

3 Pour the cake mixture into a lightly buttered loose-sided 2-lb/3-pt7½-cup French loaf tin lined with baking parchment, pressing the mixture lightly into the corners and smoothing over the top with the back of a spoon.

4 Peel and slice the reserved banana lengthways and cut the halves into six pieces. Dust them lightly with icing sugar (cut-side up) and lightly press the pieces into the surface of the cake mixture. Bake for 35 to 40 minutes until a cake skewer comes out clean. Dust lightly with icing sugar and serve cold, cut into thick slices.

light golden fruit loaf

Fresh ingredients are essential for this delicious fruit cake. Slice it and pack it away with a flask of coffee for a well-deserved break on a long car journey.

SERVES 10

175 g/6 oz/1½ sticks butter,
  softened
175 g/6 oz/scant 1 cup caster
  (superfine) sugar
3 large eggs

225 g/8 oz/2 cups plain
  (all-purpose) flour
Pinch of salt
½ tsp baking powder
140 g/5 oz/scant 1 cup golden
  sultanas (golden raisins)

55 g/2 oz/scant ½ cup
  candied peel, finely chopped
Rind of ½ lemon, finely
  grated

1 Preheat the oven to 180°C (350°F). In a mixing bowl cream together the butter and
   sugar until the mixture is light and creamy. Beat in the eggs, one at a time, beating
   well in between each addition, then fold in the flour, sifted with the salt and baking
   powder. Add the sultanas, candied peel and lemon rind and mix well.

2 Spoon the cake mixture into a lightly buttered 2-lb/3-pt/7½ cup loaf tin lined with baking parchment and smooth over the surface with the back of a spoon. Bake for 1 hour 20 minutes, but check after 1 hour, and cover with a piece of baking parchment if the top browns too quickly. Leave to cool slightly before turning out onto a wire cooling rack. Serve cold cut into slices.

organic chocolate, pistachio and banana loaf cake

Put this cake under lock and key or it will disappears in moments! The chocolate can be broken into small pieces by placing it in a plastic bag and pounding it with a rolling pin. Chopped walnuts may be substituted for pistachios.

SERVES 10

250 g/9 oz/2¼ organic plain (all-purpose) flour
2 rounded tsps baking powder
125 g/4½ oz/1 stick butter, softened
125 g/4 oz/½ cup golden caster (superfine) sugar

2 ripe organic bananas, mashed
2 large organic eggs, lightly beaten
1½ tbsps milk
½ vanilla pod (vanilla bean), split

175 g/6 oz organic dark sweet (semisweet) chocolate, crushed into small pieces
125 g/4 oz/1 cup unsalted pistachios, lightly crushed

1 Preheat the oven to 180°C (350°F). Sift the flour and baking powder into a large bowl and set aside. Beat the butter with the sugar until creamy and light. Mix in the mashed bananas, then gradually mix in the eggs and milk.

2 Using the tip of a pointed knife, split the vanilla pod and scrape out the seeds into the creamed mixture and mix them in, followed by the chocolate and pistachios. Lightly fold in the dry ingredients with a large spoon, but do not over mix.

3 Spoon the cake mixture into a lightly-buttered and floured loose-sided 2-lb/3-pt/ 7½-cup loaf tin. Bake for about 50 minutes, but check after 40 to 45 minutes, and cover with a piece of baking parchment if the top browns too quickly. The cake is ready when the top looks golden and feels firm and slightly springy to the touch. Leave to cool slightly before turning out onto a wire cooling rack.

assam tea bread

The light scent of Assam tea blends well with the dried apricots and cranberries.
Delicious freshly buttered for a mid-morning or afternoon snack.

SERVES 10

350 g/12 oz/2¼ cups dried,
   ready-soaked apricots
50 g/2 oz/⅓ cup dried
   sweetened cranberries
Juice and grated rind of 1½
   oranges

200 g/7 oz/1¼ cups soft
   brown unrefined sugar
285 ml/10 fl oz/1¼ cups hot,
   strong Assam tea
2 large eggs
150 ml/5 fl oz/⅔ cup milk

350 g/12 oz/3 cups self-
   raising (self-rising) white,
   or wholemeal (whole wheat)
   flour
1½ tbsps runny honey,
   warmed

1 Preheat the oven to 180°C (350°F). Finely chop the apricots and add them to a large
   bowl with the cranberries, orange juice, rind and sugar. Strain over the tea and mix
   lightly together. Set aside for 2½ hours to allow the ingredients to soak up the tea.

2 Beat the eggs with the milk and stir into the tea, sugar and dried fruit mixture.
   Lightly fold in the flour. Spoon the mixture into a lightly buttered 2-lb/3-pt/7½-cup
   loaf tin lined with baking parchment. Level the top with the back of a spoon.

3 Bake for about 1¼ hours. The tea bread is ready when a skewer comes out clean
   when inserted into its centre. Leave to cool slightly before turning out onto a wire
   cooling rack. Brush the warm honey over the top and serve cold cut into thin slices.

individual cherry cakes

These little cakes, made with deep red natural glacé cherries, are ideal for packing into
lunch boxes, or for a tea party when you can make an individual cake for each guest.

MAKES 8

175 g/6 oz/1½ cups self-
   raising (self-rising) flour
Pinch of salt
1 rounded tsp baking powder
85 g/3 oz/generous ½ cup
   ground almonds
175 g/6 oz/1½ sticks butter
   softened

175 g/6 oz/scant 1 cup golden
   caster (superfine) sugar
3 large eggs, lightly beaten
Rind of ½ lemon, finely
   grated
Rind of ½ orange, finely
   grated

1 tbsp cherry brandy, or
   brandy
4 tbsps freshly-squeezed
   orange juice
115 g/4 oz natural glacé
   (candied) cherries, halved

1 Preheat the oven to 170°C (325°F). Sift the flour, salt and baking powder into a mixing bowl and stir in the ground almonds. Set aside.

2 In another bowl, beat the butter and sugar until creamy. Add one egg at a time and beat until the mixture is light and creamy. Fold the lemon and orange rinds, brandy and orange juice into the dry ingredients, followed by the glacé cherries until the mixture is smooth with a consistency that will drop from the spoon when jerked slightly.

3 Fill eight non-stick small 10 x 5-cm (4 x 2-in) loaf-shaped baking tins three-quarters full and smooth the tops with the back of a spoon. Bake for about 18 minutes until well risen and golden. Leave to cool slightly before gently loosening the edges of each cake and turning them out onto a wire cooling rack.

mini french loaf cake

This small loaf cake looks pretty with a glossy black vanilla pod peeping through the baked domed cake mixture. You can of course double or triple the quantities to make two or three baby loaf cakes.

MAKES 1

55 g/2 oz/generous ¼ cup caster (superfine) sugar
55 g/2 oz/½ cup self-raising (self-rising) flour, sifted
Small pinch of salt

55 g/2 oz/½ stick butter
2 small eggs
25 g/1 oz/¼ cup almonds, finely ground
½ vanilla pod, split

2 tbsps quince jelly or sieved apricot jam (jelly), to glaze
Icing (confectioner's) sugar, to dust

1 Mix the sugar, sifted flour and salt together in a bowl. Melt but do not brown the butter and set aside to cool.

2 Lightly beat the eggs and mix them into the sugar and flour mixture and gradually add the cooled butter, ground almonds and the vanilla pod seeds (reserving the empty pod). Mix well but not too vigorously. Cover and refrigerate for 30 minutes to 1 hour.

3 Preheat the oven to 190°C (375°F). Spoon the mixture into a lightly buttered ½-lb/¾-pt/2-cup French loaf tin lined at the base with baking parchment and level the top with the back of a spoon. Lay the reserved split vanilla pod on top of the mixture and bake for 25 minutes until the cake looks lightly golden and domed with the pod peeping through the cooked cake mixture.

4 If you wish to glaze the cake, gently melt 2 tablespoons of quince jelly or sieved apricot jam until syrupy and brush it warm over the top. Leave to set and serve, cut in thin delicate slices arranged on a tea plate, lightly dusted with icing sugar.

sweet marrow bread

Marrow bread will last for one week kept in an airtight tin and freezes well for future occasions. The quantities in this recipe make three breads.

ONE BREAD SERVES 10

200 ml/7 fl oz/scant 1 cup olive oil
450 g/1 lb/3 cups soft brown sugar
3 large eggs
3 tsps pure vanilla extract
1 tbsp black treacle (dark molasses) or golden syrup (light corn syrup)
650 g/1 lb 7 oz grated marrow flesh
350 g/12 oz/2 cups raisins mixed with sultanas (golden raisins)
115 g/4 oz/generous 1 cup flaked (slivered) almonds, (optional)
500 g/1lb 2 oz/4½ cups self-raising (self-rising) flour, sifted
1 tsp salt
1 tbsp mixed spice (allspice)

1 Preheat the oven to 150°C (300°F). Lightly butter and line three 2-lb/3-pt/7½-cup loaf tins. In the bowl of an electric mixer, beat together the olive oil and sugar and slowly incorporate the eggs, beating well until the mixture forms a batter-like consistency. Beat in the vanilla extract, treacle or golden syrup and the grated marrow flesh, then stir in the dried fruits and the flaked almonds, if using. Lightly fold in the flour, salt and mixed spice, sifted together then divide the cake batter between the three tins.

2 Bake for about 1 hour 45 minutes. Leave to cool in the tins for 10 minutes before carefully turning out onto wire cooling racks. Once cold, the bread will freeze well wrapped in plastic freezer bags.

organic chocolate roulade

This textured roulade makes an appealing winter cake dusted with icing sugar and decorated with winter berries. You will need a large, lined 25 x 40-cm (10 x 16-in) roulade tin. An oven roasting tray of about the same dimensions, lined with baking parchment cut slightly larger than the tin makes a good substitute.

SERVES 8

FOR THE SPONGE
5 large organic eggs, separated
140 g/5 oz/¾ cup organic caster (superfine) sugar
225 g (½ lb) dark (semisweet) organic chocolate

1 tsp strong organic instant coffee, mixed with 100 ml/ 3½ fl oz/½ cup hot water

FOR THE FILLING
300 ml/10 fl oz/1½ cups organic double (heavy) cream

1 tsp vanilla extract, or pure vanilla bean paste
2 tsps organic golden caster (superfine) sugar

Icing (confectioner's) sugar, to dust

1 Preheat the oven to 200°C (400°F). To make the sponge, beat the egg yolks until very pale, using an electric beater on medium speed. Gradually add the sugar and beat until thick and creamy.

2 In a separate spotlessly clean mixing bowl, beat the egg whites until quite stiff. Meanwhile, melt the chocolate broken into small pieces with the coffee in a mixing bowl over a pan of hot water taken off the heat and mix until completely melted. Stir the chocolate liquid into the egg yolks and sugar mixture until evenly mixed.

3 Using a large spoon, fold about two tablespoons of the whisked egg white into the chocolate mixture to loosen it before gently and gradually folding in the remaining egg whites.

4 Pour the mixture into the prepared tin, levelling the surface with the back of a spoon. Bake for 13 minutes until the sponge is slightly browned and firm to the touch. Slide the sponge and parchment out of the tin onto a wire cooling rack and cover immediately with a clean, damp tea cloth (this prevents the cake from cracking too much). Leave to cool at room temperature for the best part of the day, but preferably overnight.

5 To make the filling, beat the filling ingredients together to form fairly stiff peaks. Using a spatula, gently spread the mixture over the sponge and roll it up with the help of the baking parchment, carefully pulling the paper from the sponge as you do so. Set on a flat serving plate with the seam underneath. Dust lightly with icing sugar and serve, cut into thick slices.

classic raspberry swiss roll

The filling options for this classic Swiss roll range from buttercream, whipped cream, home-made jam or lemon curd. Finish with a fine sugary coating of golden caster sugar which adds a light caramelized flavour to the sponge cake.

SERVES 6

FOR THE SPONGE
3 large eggs
115 g/4 oz/generous ½ cup
 caster (superfine) sugar
1 tbsp warm water

115 g/4 oz/1 cup self-raising
 (self-rising) flour, sifted
Pinch of salt
25 g/1 oz/scant ¼ cup golden
 caster (superfine) sugar

FOR THE FILLING
340 g/12 oz/1½ cups
 raspberry jam (jelly)
One quantity of raspberry
 buttercream (see page 10)

1 Preheat the oven to 200°C (400°F). Whisk the eggs until blended, then add the sugar and continue to whisk until the mixture is thick and creamy. Lightly stir in the warm water, then gently fold in the sifted flour and salt, making sure not to over mix.

2 Pour the mixture into a buttered 30 x-20 (12 x 8-in) Swiss roll tin lined with baking parchment and lightly tap the tin to level the mixture. Bake for 11 minutes, until the sponge is well risen and lightly golden.

3 Lay a clean kitchen towel on a work surface. Place a sheet of baking parchment over it and sift the caster sugar over the paper. Remove the sponge from the oven and carefully loosen the edges. Turn it out onto the sugar-coated paper and carefully peel away the baking parchment.

4 Roll up the sponge with the sugared paper while it is still warm, then carefully transfer it onto a wire cooling rack with the seam underneath. When it has cooled, unroll the sponge and spread it thickly and evenly with the jam and buttercream, leaving a spare 2-cm (¾-in) margin at the edges clear.

5 Roll up the sponge with the help of the sugared paper pulling it away from the sponge as it is rolled when the jam and buttercream will spread out towards the edges. Trim the end pieces with a sharp knife just before serving to keep the inside of the sponge fresh and moist. Transfer the roulade to a flat serving plate with the seam underneath and serve in thick slices.

chestnut and marrons glacés roulade

This delicious sponge spiralled around a creamy chestnut filling and finished with a chocolate and chestnut covering is great for special occasions. You can add extra chopped marrons glacés to the filling and decorate the top with almonds.

SERVES 6 TO 7

FOR THE SPONGE
4 large eggs
100 g/3½ oz/generous ½ cup
  caster (superfine) sugar
100 g/3½ oz/scant 1 cup
  plain (all-purpose) flour
Pinch of salt
1 tbsp warm water
1 tsp rosewater, warmed
Icing (confectioner's) sugar,
  to dust

FOR THE FILLING AND TOPPING
225 g/8 oz/1 cup tinned
  unsweetened chestnut purée
115 g/4 oz/generous ½ cup
  caster (superfine) sugar

150 g (5½ oz) dark
  (semisweet) chocolate
250 ml/9 fl oz/generous 1 cup
  fresh double (heavy) cream

Icing (confectioner's) sugar,
  to dust

1 Preheat the oven to 190°C (375°F). To make the sponge, whisk the eggs and sugar until thick and pale and the whisk leaves a heavy trail when lifted. Sift the flour and salt into the mixture and fold in gently with the warm water and rosewater.

2 Pour the mixture into a lightly buttered 30 x 12-cm (12 x 8-in) Swiss roll tin lined with baking parchment and level the top with the back of a large spoon. Bake for 12 to 14 minutes, until golden and firm to the touch.

3 Lay a clean kitchen towel on a work surface. Place a sheet of baking parchment over it and sift the icing sugar over the paper. Remove the sponge from the oven and carefully loosen the edges. Turn it out onto the sugar-coated paper and carefully peel away the baking parchment. Roll up the sponge with the sugared paper while it is still warm then carefully transfer it onto a wire cooling rack with the seam underneath.

4 To make the filling, gently warm the chestnut purée in a small saucepan over a low heat, using a spoon to mix in the sugar and break up the lumps. Remove from the heat and transfer it to a mixing bowl. Set aside.

5 Melt the chocolate broken into small pieces in a mixing bowl over a pan of hot water taken off the heat stirring until melted. Whip the cream until it forms soft peaks then fold it into the cooled chestnut purée. Divide the cream and chestnut mixture in two and mix the melted chocolate into one of the batches. Set this aside for the topping.

6 When it has cooled, unroll the sponge and spread evenly with the pale chestnut cream filling, leaving a spare 2-cm (¾-in) margin at the edges clear. Roll up the sponge with the help of the sugared paper pulling it away from the sponge as it is rolled when the filling will spread out towards the edges. Refrigerate for 30 minutes then cover evenly with the topping. Leave to set then transfer the roulade to a flat serving plate with the seam underneath and dust with icing sugar before serving.

biscuits and meringues

The word biscuit comes from the French bis-cuit, or twice-baked. Each country has its own speciality varying in shape, size and texture. The French have *langues de chats* – thin, crisp biscuits, whereas the Italians are famous for their almond-flavoured *amaretti*. The Dutch favour dark spicy biscuits made from a slightly heavy paste of flour, honey and ginger, often prettily impressed with a variety of shapes and symbols, whilst the Americans like their biscuits fat, and simply bursting with chocolate drops, pecans, raisins, maple syrup – you name it!

There are hundreds of varieties of commercially-made biscuits to choose from, baked to the same colour, shaped to the same form and in beautiful packaging. With few exceptions, however, the best biscuits come from our own kitchens, where they can be made from fine, fresh ingredients and eaten warm from the oven.

Meringues have a special affinity with cream and are lovely eaten with summer fruits. They can be glamorized by lightly tinting the beaten egg whites with food colouring before baking them. Meringues also add a delicious sweet note to an afternoon tea, but don't just relegate them to summer eating – they are just as nice in winter mixed with cranberries and orange peel or made with soft brown sugar to give them a warm, golden colour and slightly denser texture to go with stoned fruits like damsons or plums.

hazelnut and ginger biscotti

No excuses required for dunking these twice-baked Italian specialities into a caffé latte. Keep them stored in an airtight container to keep them fresh for up to one week.

MAKES 14

125 g/4½ oz/1 stick unsalted (sweet) butter, softened
160 g/5¾ oz/¾ cup golden caster (superfine) sugar

Thumb-size piece of fresh root ginger (gingerroot), peeled and finely grated
300 g/10½ oz/2½ cups plain (all-purpose) flour
1½ tsp baking powder

Pinch of salt
1 tsp ground ginger
2 tbsps maple syrup
100 g/3½ oz/scant 1 cup whole hazelnuts

1 Preheat the oven to 180°C (350°F). Beat the softened butter with the sugar until pale and creamy. Add the fresh ginger, flour, baking powder and salt and ground ginger and mix together. Add the maple syrup, 1 tablespoon of water and the nuts and mix thoroughly.

2 Tip the mixture onto a baking sheet lined with baking parchment and shape it into a 15 x 23-cm (6 x 9-in) sausage. Bake for 30 minutes then remove from the oven and turn onto a wire cooling rack. When cooled, cut the sausage into 1-cm (½-in) slices with a sharp bread knife. Place the slices onto a baking sheet and return to the oven for a further 7 to 8 minutes to dry them out and colour them slightly.

vanilla and lemon shortbread

Shortbread is so called because of its high butter content which gives it a 'short', crisp texture. The hint of lemon zest and vanilla seeds deliciously scent this tender shortbread.

MAKES 8

125 g/4 oz/1 stick butter
90 g/3 oz/½ cup golden caster (superfine) sugar
Rind of ½ lemon, finely grated

½ vanilla pod (vanilla bean)
200 g/6½ oz/1½ cups plain (all-purpose) flour

Extra golden caster (superfine) sugar, for sprinkling

1 Cream together the butter, sugar and lemon rind in a mixing bowl. Using the tip of a pointed knife, split the vanilla pod and scrape out the seeds directly into the creamed mixture. Mix in the seeds, then lightly fold the sifted flour into the mixture until it turns into a soft dough.

2 Knead the dough lightly on a floured board until smooth. Very lightly flour a round 17-cm (7-in) shortbread mould, then carefully roll the dough into a circle about the same size as the mould. Gently press the dough into the mould and press the edges out with your fingertips to fit the mould exactly. If you do not have a mould, shape the dough into a neat circle of the above dimensions. Prick the surface with a fork, then with the blade of a knife, make four shallow cuts across the width of the circle, to resemble the spokes of a wheel. Carefully unmould the shortbread onto a baking sheet and refrigerate for 1 hour.

3 Preheat the oven to 160°C (325°F). Remove the dough from the fridge and bake for about 30 minutes, until lightly golden. Lightly dredge with sugar while the biscuit is still warm.

rolled cookies

Here I have enriched the basic vanilla and lemon shortbread dough (see page 121) with a choice of tempting flavourings. Simply add the flavouring ingredients to the biscuit dough. Kitchenware shops supply some great biscuit cutter shapes, like the butterfly and flower ones used for these biscuits.

MAKES 40 BISCUITS USING TWO OF THE FOLLOWING FLAVOURINGS

One quantity of biscuit dough
  (see page 121)

Icing (confectioner's) sugar,
  for dusting

pistachio biscuits
40 g/1½ oz/scant ½ cup organic pistachios,
  roughly chopped
½ tsp almond or pistachio essence into a half
  quantity of shortbread biscuit paste

glacé cherry biscuits
55 g/2 oz/⅓ cup natural red glacé (candied)
  cherries
10 finely chopped pistachio nuts mixed
  in for extra colour

candied peel and lemon
40 g/1½ oz candied peel, finely chopped
½ orange, finely grated

chocolate and hazelnut
40 g/1½ oz dark (semisweet) chocolate
28 g/1 oz/¼ cup crushed roasted hazelnuts

1 Remove the chilled shortbread dough from the fridge and cut it into two equal portions. Knead each portion lightly until smooth, then incorporate one of the above flavourings into each piece.

2 Roll each flavoured portion into a smooth ball then form the balls into two fat sausages 6 cm (2½ in) long. Lay two small sheets of baking parchment on top of a clean work surface and dust them lightly with icing sugar. Roll each sausage in the paper and place them in a plastic bag. Chill for about one hour. Remove from the fridge and slice the rolls into thin discs. You could also roll out the dough to a ½-cm (¼-in) thickness and stamp out different shapes with decorative biscuit cutters.

3 Bake them in a preheated oven at 160°C (325°F) for about 5 to 8 minutes, until pale golden around the edges.

kaffir lime macaroons

Fragrant Asian flavourings make these fluffy, soft-centred macaroons an unusual coffee-time treat. A few thin strips of fresh or dried kaffir lime leaves on top of the macaroons add an attractive finish. Lime zest or finely chopped candied orange can substitute for kaffir lime leaves if preferred.

MAKES 16

3 medium egg whites
115 g/4 oz/scant 1 cup icing
  (confectioner's) sugar, sifted
115 g/4 oz/scant 1 cup
  ground almonds

115 g/4 oz/1½ cups
  desiccated coconut (dry
  unsweetened coconut)
Rind of ½ unwaxed lemon,
  finely grated

1½ tbsps rum
4 fresh kaffir lime leaves, cut
  into paper-thin strips
Edible rice paper
Icing (confectioner's) sugar,
  to dust

TIP

These macaroons are best eaten the same day they are baked, as their texture tends to soften when stored for any length of time. However, you can regain their former freshly-baked texture – which should be crisp on the outside and soft and chewy on the inside – by placing them briefly in a warm to moderate oven for a few minutes just before serving.

1   Preheat the oven to 150°C (300°F). Whisk the egg whites in a large mixing bowl until stiff. Gently fold in half the icing sugar and half the ground almonds, then fold in the remaining icing sugar, ground almonds, desiccated coconut, lemon rind, rum and kaffir lime leaves. Fold lightly together until the mixture is evenly blended.

2   Transfer the mixture into a piping bag fitted with a large plain nozzle and pipe the mixture into whirls the size of large walnuts on a baking sheet lined with edible rice paper. Slightly flatten each shape with your fingers, and dust with icing sugar.

3   Bake for about 17 to 18 minutes, until golden on the outside and soft inside. Leave on a wire cooling rack to cool, then gently tear away the excess rice paper from the edges of the macaroons before serving. Dust lightly with icing sugar.

rolled almond biscuits

This almond paste is ideal for making these very delicate biscuits which are rolled into cigar shapes while still warm and pliable. They are great served with mousse or sorbets.

MAKES 14 SMALL OR 9 TO 10 LARGE BISCUITS

25 g/1 oz marzipan
80 g/3 oz/½ cup caster
  (superfine) sugar

Few drops of vanilla extract
1 large egg, lightly beaten
65 g/2½ oz/½ cup plain
  (all-purpose) flour

Pinch of salt
1½ tbsps double (heavy)
  cream

1   Roughly chop the marzipan into small cubes and mix it together with the sugar, vanilla and egg. Cream the ingredients with a large spoon or with an electric beater set at low speed so that the mixture does not become frothy. Stir in the flour and salt until the mixture is smooth. Cover and refrigerate for 1 hour, then stir in the cream.

2   Preheat the oven to 180°C (350°F). In pencil, draw four 10-cm (4-in) circles on the underside of a sheet of baking parchment. Place the parchment on a baking sheet and very thinly spread 1 teaspoon of the paste into these circles.

3   Bake for 4 minutes until the edges look slightly golden. While they are still warm, roll the circles carefully into cigars. Repeat until the paste is finished. For larger biscuits, add a little more paste to a circle about 15 cm (6 in) in diameter.

iced star biscuits

For a festive finish, add a frosty white icing and tiny silver balls to the surface of the biscuits. Make a little hole with a skewer at the tip of each of the uncooked biscuits and when they are baked and decorated they can be laced with thin ribbons.

MAKES 25

FOR THE BISCUIT PASTE
225 g/8 oz/2 cups plain
  (all-purpose) flour
140 g/5 oz/1¼ sticks butter
125 g/4½ oz/¾ cup caster
  (superfine) sugar
Pinch of salt

2 tsps pure vanilla bean paste
  or pure vanilla extract
Rind of ½ large unwaxed
  lemon, finely grated
½ tsp fresh mixed spice
  (allspice)
2 medium egg yolks

FOR THE LEMON ICING
1 egg white
2 tsps fresh lemon juice
250 g/9 oz/scant 2 cups icing
  (confectioner's) sugar,
  double sifted
Edible silver balls

1 Sift the flour onto a board or marble slab. Make an open well in the centre and into it place the butter, sugar, salt, vanilla, lemon rind, spice and egg yolks. Draw the fingers of one hand together and, lightly and quickly, work the ingredients with a bird-like pecking motion until the mixture resembles scrambled eggs. Gradually draw in the flour and, using the same finger movement, quickly combine the remaining ingredients to form a crumb-like mixture. Gather together and lightly press the moist crumbs into a soft ball.

2 Lightly knead the dough by pushing it away from you with the heel of your hand and drawing it back 4 to 5 times until the dough is smooth. This may be easier to do by cutting the dough into two sections and kneading each separately. Wrap in a plastic bag and refrigerate for 1 hour.

3 Roll out the dough onto a lightly floured board until it is ½ cm (¼ in) thick, then using a 7-cm (3-in) star-shaped biscuit cutter, stamp out the biscuits. Using a palette knife, carefully transfer them onto a lightly-buttered baking sheet and refrigerate for 20 minutes.

4 Preheat the oven to 160° C (325° F). Remove the tray from the fridge and place it in the oven for 9 to 10 minutes until the biscuits are pale golden around the edges. Leave to cool slightly then transfer them to a wire cooling rack.

5 To make the icing, lightly beat the egg white until light and fluffy in a large mixing bowl. Add the lemon juice, then gradually add the icing sugar, beating well between each addition until you get a smooth shiny paste. Brush the icing carefully over the surface of the biscuits and while the icing is still liquid, dot over the silver balls.

ricciarello biscuits

These moist, chewy-centred Tuscan biscuits are baked and finished with a dusting of icing sugar. In Italy, there are many secret recipes for these small biscuits: some are made with sugar and honey, others with vanilla or lemon zest. Add one or two teaspoons of rum or amaretto to make them a touch boozy.

MAKES 20

200 g/7 oz/1½ cups ground almonds
225 g/8 oz/1 cup white or golden caster (superfine) sugar

1 large egg white
1 or 2 tsps rum or amaretto liqueur
1 tsp orange or clementine zest, finely grated

1 tsp pure vanilla bean paste or vanilla extract
Edible rice paper
Icing (confectioner's) sugar, to dust

1 Preheat the oven to 110°C (225°F). Sift the almonds and sugar into a mixing bowl. Whisk the egg white to make a light froth, then lightly mix it into the dry ingredients, adding the rum or amaretto, zest and vanilla.

2 Divide the paste into 20 pieces the size and shape of a walnut. Flatten the shapes lightly with the flat side of a knife to form little oval shapes.

3 Line a baking sheet with edible rice paper and dust it with icing sugar. Place the shaped biscuit dough on top, spacing them a little apart and bake for 30 to 35 minutes, until the biscuits are firm to the touch and very pale golden around the edges. The surface of the biscuits will form little cracks as they bake, and they look particularly attractive finished with a dusting of icing sugar as they cool.

truffle and amaretto slice

This dense, rich truffle biscuit goes deliciously with coffee. Pistachio nuts add flavour and colour. For a natural, simple presentation, serve in thin slices straight from the freezer.

MAKES 12 SLICES

280 g/10 oz dark (semisweet) chocolate, preferably Valrhona
225 g/8 oz/2 sticks butter
1 tbsp water
1 tbsp caster (superfine) sugar

2 tbsps amaretto liqueur or rum (optional)
2 tsps orange-flavoured liqueur
2 egg yolks
85 g/3 oz amaretti biscuits
115 g/4 oz/$\frac{2}{3}$ cup glacé

(candied) cherries, halved
Sifted icing (confectioner's) sugar, mixed with cocoa powder (unsweetened cocoa) for a slightly bitter flavour, or chocolate powder for a sweeter finish, to dust

1 Break the chocolate into small pieces and place it in a bowl over a pan of hot water taken off the heat. Add the butter, water and sugar and stir until smooth. Remove the bowl from the pan and set aside to cool.

2 Lightly whisk in the liqueurs followed by the egg yolks. Finely crush half the amaretti to a fine powder and stir into the chocolate mixture. Cut the remaining biscuits into quarters, folding them into the mixture with the glacé cherries until well covered.

3 Lightly butter and line a 20 x 13-cm (8 x 5-in) tin 7½ cm (3 in) deep. Pour the mixture into the tin while it is still fairly fluid and refrigerate for at least 5 or 6 hours, or better still overnight.

4 Remove the contents from the tin and dust liberally with icing sugar, then peel away the baking parchment. Use a very sharp knife to cut the slab into thin slices. Keep chilled until required as it softens if kept for any length of time at room temperature.

meringue iced almond biscuits

These unusual Italian biscuits are iced with a simple meringue mixture before baking and are designed to melt in the mouth.

MAKES 35

4 large egg whites
350 g/12 oz/2½ cups icing (confectioner's) sugar, sifted, plus extra to dust
1 tsp grated nutmeg
1 tsp ground cinnamon
450 g/1 lb/3¼ cups ground almonds
Juice of ½ lemon

1 Place the egg whites in a bowl and whisk until stiff. Gradually fold in the icing sugar and the nutmeg and cinnamon. Beat together for 30 seconds until the mixture is smooth and forms a dropping consistency.

2 Reserve six tablespoons of the mixture. Continue to beat the remaining mixture for five minutes. Stir in the ground almonds and lemon juice and mix to a smooth paste. Wrap in a plastic bag and chill for 30 minutes. Preheat the oven to 200°C (400°F).

3 Dust a clean work surface with icing sugar and roll the paste out to 2 cm (¾ in) deep. Cut the dough with a 4-cm (1½-in) round biscuit cutter and place the shapes on buttered baking sheets, spaced a little apart. Bake for 6 or 7 minutes, until lightly browned, then remove from the oven.

4 Reduce the oven temperature to 180°C (350°F). Loosen the biscuits slightly and brush the reserved meringue mixture over the surface of the biscuits. Return the biscuits to the oven and leave them to cook for about 5 minutes until the meringue is crisp but uncoloured. Place on a wire cooling rack to cool. They store well in an airtight container for several days.

heart-shaped biscuits

These are fun, perhaps for a wedding or as a simple biscuit garnish to summer or warm poached fruits. Warm them in the oven, particularly if serving with poached fruits.

MAKES 28

One quantity of rich sweet pastry (see page 12) with an extra 25 g/1 oz/scant ¼ cup of caster (superfine) sugar and an extra tsp of vanilla extract, chilled
3–4 drops red food colouring
Egg glaze (see page 9)

1 Cut the chilled dough into two equal pieces. Place one piece into a plastic bag and return it to the fridge. Colour a walnut-size piece of dough pink using the red food colouring. Knead it into the dough until it is evenly coloured pink. Divide in two.

2 Remove the uncoloured piece of dough from the fridge and divide it into two equal pieces. Roll the four pieces into oblong shapes about ½ cm (¼ in) thick and paint each strip with egg glaze. Alternately layer the uncoloured and coloured pieces on top of one another and press to seal. Cut the slab in half lengthways and place one half on top of the other, sealing with egg glaze. Place the layered slab (made up of eight pink and white layers) onto a lightly floured board and chill for 15 minutes.

3 Remove the dough from the fridge and cut it into 1-cm (½-in) thick slices. Using a heart-shaped biscuit cutter, stamp out the biscuits, rolling the dough a little larger to fit the cutter size, if necessary. Transfer the shapes to a lightly-buttered baking sheet and refrigerate for 20 minutes. Preheat the oven to 190ºC (375ºF).

4 Bake for 6 minutes then remove from the oven, leave to cool slightly and lightly brush the surface of each biscuit with egg glaze. Return to the oven for a further 2 minutes to give the surface of the biscuits a pretty shine.

iced almond and pine nut biscuits

These petits fours can be iced or finished with a simple dusting of icing sugar to emphasize the contours of the nut topping. If you prefer a coffee-flavoured icing, substitute the orange flower water and zest with a few drops of coffee essence or strong diluted coffee.

MAKES 15

FOR THE BISCUIT MIX
100 g/3¹⁄₂ oz/³⁄₄ cup ground almonds
140 g/5 oz/³⁄₄ cup caster (superfine) sugar
3 egg whites, lightly whisked
115 g/4 oz/1 cup pine nuts

FOR THE ORANGE-SCENTED ICING
225 g/8 oz/generous 1¹⁄₂ cups icing (confectioner's) sugar, double sifted
Few drops orange flower water
1 tsp finely grated orange zest
1 egg white, lightly whisked

1   Preheat the oven to 230ºC (450ºF). Mix the almonds and sugar together with two of the egg whites to make a moist, pliable paste. Form the paste into walnut-size balls.

2   Lay the pine nuts out on a plate. Dip each ball in the remaining egg white and roll them in the pine nuts until evenly coated. Place the balls in small petits fours paper cases and place them on a baking sheet. Bake for 5 to 6 minutes until the nuts are very lightly coloured, then transfer on a wire cooling rack.

3   To make the icing, mix the icing sugar, flower water and orange zest with enough egg white to achieve a smooth, dropping consistency, then quickly drizzle the icing from a spoon in a zig-zag pattern over the tops of the biscuits. Leave to set.

marshmallow meringue cake with fruits

The meringue's contrasting textures, which range from a crisp outer coating to a soft, almost marshmallow centre, are made by adding vinegar and cornflour to the beaten egg whites. Allow to rest for 45 minutes before serving to allow the flavours and textures to merge.

SERVES 6

FOR THE FRUITS
5 juicy clementines
2½ tbsps caster (superfine) sugar
2 ripe passion fruit

FOR THE MERINGUE
4 large egg whites
225 g/8 oz/1½ cups icing (confectioner's) sugar, sifted

1 tsp cornflour (cornstarch), sifted
1 tsp white wine vinegar

FOR THE FILLING
285 ml/10 fl oz/1¼ cups double (heavy) cream
3 level tbsps golden caster (superfine) sugar, or to taste
425 ml/15 fl oz/scant 2 cups vanilla yoghurt

TO DECORATE
6 marshmallows, quartered
Extra passion fruit, sliced
Icing (confectioner's) sugar, to dust
Sprigs of redcurrants

1   Start by preparing the fruits. Peel and separate the clementines into segments and remove any of the white pith. Add them to a mixing bowl with the sugar. Cut the passion fruit into halves and squeeze the juice and seeds over the fruit. Mix lightly together and set aside.

2   Preheat the oven to 140°C (275°F). To make the meringue, place the egg whites in a spotlessly clean large mixing bowl and beat them until stiff with an electric beater. Add the sifted icing sugar 2 tablespoons at a time, making sure to beat well in between each addition, until all the sugar is used up and the meringue looks thick and glossy. Quickly fold in the cornflour and vinegar until well combined, but do not over mix or the meringue will lose its volume.

3   Using a metal spoon, spread the meringue mixture in a 25-cm (10-in) circle onto a baking sheet lined with baking parchment and form a hollow in the centre. Bake for 1 hour then turn off the heat and leave the meringue inside the oven until cool.

4   In the meantime, make the filling. Beat the cream and sugar until it forms soft but firm peaks, then mix in the yoghurt. When the meringue has cooled, transfer it to a serving dish, pile the filling into the centre of the meringue cake and spoon over the reserved fruits. Sprinkle over the marshmallow pieces. Add extra slices of passion fruit and dust with icing sugar. Serve cut into tall magnificent slices decorated with sprigs of fresh redcurrants and an extra dusting of icing sugar.

pistachio and cinnamon biscuits

Use a wooden biscuit mould to shape the biscuits. If you don't have one, stamp out rounds with a fluted biscuit cutter or a serrated-edged ravioli cutter, then impress a small decorative pattern over the surface of the uncooked biscuits.

MAKES 16

115 g/4 oz/1 cup whole blanched almonds
85 g/3 oz/¾ cup pistachios
100 g/3½ oz/scant 1 cup plain (all-purpose) flour

1 large egg
25 g/1 oz/¼ stick butter, softened
40 g/1½ oz/scant ¼ cup caster (superfine) sugar

2 tbsps clear runny honey
1 tbsp rum or rosewater
1 tsp ground cinnamon
Icing (confectioner's) sugar, to dust

1 Preheat the oven to 160°C (325°F). Put the almonds and pistachios in a food processor and whiz them into a fine, slightly crumbly pale green powder.

2 In a large mixing bowl, mix together the flour, egg, butter, sugar, honey and ground nuts then add the rum or rosewater and cinnamon to form a fairly stiff paste that holds its shape.

3 Sift some flour onto a clean work surface and divide the mixture into 16 pieces. With lightly-floured hands, roll each piece into a smooth shape to fit your chosen mould. Press each piece of dough into the mould then gently pull it away to reveal the impression.

4 Arrange the shapes set apart onto a very lightly buttered baking sheet lined with baking parchment and bake for 8 to 10 minutes, or until the biscuits are slightly brown around the edges. Serve warm and lightly dusted with icing sugar to emphasize the delicate texture of these pretty biscuits.

stripy chocolate and vanilla cookies

These delicious cookies will give your kitchen such an enticing sweet chocolate aroma, that everyone will be inviting themselves in for coffee!

MAKES 25

140 g/5 oz/1¼ sticks butter, softened
70 g/2½ oz/½ cup icing (confectioner's) sugar, sifted
Pinch of salt

200 g/7 oz/1⅔ cups plain (all-purpose) flour, sifted
15 g/½ oz/2 tbsps cocoa powder (unsweetened cocoa), sifted

1 tsp vanilla extract, or the seeds from 1 vanilla pod (vanilla bean), or 1 tsp pure vanilla bean paste
Egg glaze (see page 9)

1 Beat the butter with the icing sugar and salt until pale and creamy. Lightly knead in the flour and divide the dough into two equal portions. Knead the cocoa powder into one of the portions until evenly coloured and the vanilla into the other portion. Form each portion into a moist ball then wrap separately in plastic wrap. Leave to firm up in the fridge for 25 minutes.

2 Divide each piece of dough into four pieces and roll each piece into a long, thin strip about 7½-cm (3-in) wide and ½-cm (¼-in) thick. Stack one on top of the other in alternate colours and seal each layer with egg glaze. Return the layered slab to the fridge for 15 minutes to chill. Preheat the oven to 190°C (375°F).

3 Remove the dough from the fridge. Tidy up the sides with a sharp knife then, starting from one end, cut ½-cm (¼-in) slices. Place the slices, spaced apart, onto a lightly-buttered baking sheet and bake for about 5 or 6 minutes, or until the biscuits start to look lightly golden around the edges.

sugar pink meringues

As in the giant Italian meringues recipe (see page 140), this method of beating whites with icing sugar in a bowl set over a pan of simmering water gives a firmer and more durable result than simply folding in the sugar. If you prefer ivory white meringues, omit the food colouring.

MAKES 10

FOR THE MERINGUE
4 large egg whites
250 g/9 oz/scant 2 cups icing (confectioner's) sugar, sifted
3–4 drops of scarlet food colouring

FOR THE FILLING
285 ml/10 fl oz/1¼ cups double (heavy) cream, chilled
1 tsp pure vanilla extract
1 level tbsp caster (superfine) sugar

1 Preheat the oven to 120°C (250°F). Whisk the egg whites with the sugar in a mixing bowl set over a pan of simmering water until thick and very creamy. Remove from the heat. Add the food colouring to a teaspoon and drop the colouring from the teaspoon into the meringue mixture (adding the colouring to the teaspoon first avoids dropping more food colouring than necessary into the meringue). Fold it lightly into the meringue until evenly coloured to a soft pink, making sure not to over mix.

2 Fill a piping bag fitted with a six-star nozzle with the mixture. Pipe it into small, uniform whirls onto a large baking sheet lined with baking parchment, spacing them a little apart. Bake for 1 to 1¼ hours. If the meringues do not peel away easily from the parchment, return them to the oven for a further 10 minutes. Place on a wire cooling rack.

3 To make the filling, add the cream, vanilla and sugar to a large mixing bowl and beat the cream until it forms firm but not stiff peaks. Fill the piping bag fitted with a six-star or plain nozzle with the cream and carefully fill the meringues about 30 minutes before serving them. The crisp meringue shells (without the cream filling), will store layered between silicone paper in an airtight tin for several weeks.

chocolate meringue snowballs

These little fluffy clouds of meringue are enriched with a surprise centre of rich chocolate and hazelnuts. Almond chocolate with whole nuts may also be used.

MAKES 16 TO 18

4 large egg whites
225 g/8 oz/generous 1 cup
  caster (superfine) sugar

85 g/3 oz hazelnut chocolate
  with whole nuts

1 Preheat the oven to 110ºC (225ºF). Put the egg whites into a large, spotlessly clean mixing bowl and beat them until they form stiff peaks firm enough to hold their own shape. Mix 1 tbsp of the sugar into the meringue and beat for a further minute until a whisk drawn through the meringue holds a peak that is upright and unbending. Lightly fold half the sugar (see tip) into the egg whites followed by the remaining half but don't over mix or you will lose the meringue's volume.

2 Place the hazelnut chocolate in a plastic bag and crush it roughly with a rolling pin into small 1-cm (½-in) pieces. Remove 16 to 18 of the small pieces and set them aside. Crush the remaining chocolate into a fine powder. Lightly sprinkle half the finer chocolate bits over the surface of the meringue.

3 Using an ice cream scoop, take a round of the chocolate meringue mixture and while it is still in the scoop, press a small piece of the broken nut chocolate into the centre. Run a teaspoon between the scoop and the meringue and ease it out onto a baking sheet lined with baking parchment. Make 16 to 17 more rounds in the same way spreading them a little apart (you will need two baking sheets). Bake for one hour, or until the meringues peel away from the baking parchment without resistance.

TIP

This meringue mixture uses a lot of sugar so to avoid losing the valuable air beaten into the egg whites, gently transfer the meringue to one side of the mixing bowl and, using a large metal spoon, add the sugar to the other side. Fold the sugar into the meringue from the side of the bowl in a gentle lifting and folding movement until just combined.

sweet potato and maple syrup flapjacks

Sweet potato combined with maple syrup, ginger and pecans make these chewey biscuits a popular treat with children and adults alike.

MAKES 8 WEDGES

115 g/4 oz sweet potato
70 g/2½ oz/½ stick butter
75 ml/2½ fl oz/¼ cup maple
  syrup

25 g/1 oz/¼ cup soft, light
  brown sugar
140 g/5 oz/generous 1¼ cups
  flaked oats

1 tsp ground ginger
70 g/2½ oz/½ cup pecans or
  walnuts, chopped

1 Preheat the oven to 160ºC (325ºF). Peel and grate the sweet potato and set aside. Melt the butter in a medium-size saucepan, then stir in the maple syrup followed by the sugar. Add the grated sweet potato and leave to simmer gently for 3 to 4 minutes. Add the remaining ingredients, and stir until thoroughly combined.

2 Spoon the flapjack mixture into a lightly buttered 20-cm (8-in) round loose-bottomed sandwich tin lined with baking parchment. Level the top with a large palette knife and bake in the oven for 40 to 50 minutes. Leave to cool, then cut into slices.

giant italian meringues

These billowy clouds of crisp, Italian meringue make unusual presents packed in cellophane and ribbon. You can scatter flaked almonds over the tops of the meringues instead of the strips of orange.

MAKES 4

4 large egg whites
250 g/9 oz/scant 2 cups icing
  (confectioner's) sugar
1 tsp vanilla extract

50 g/2 oz/scant ³/₄ cup fresh
  cranberries
1 tbsp strips of orange rind
  from a jar of marmalade

15 g/¹/₂ oz/scant ¹/₃ cup flaked
  almonds, (optional)

1 Preheat the oven to 120°C (250°F). Whisk the egg whites with the icing sugar and vanilla extract in a bowl over a pan of simmering water until thick and very creamy. Make sure the bottom of the bowl does not touch the water. Remove the bowl from the pan.

2 Lightly butter a large baking sheet and line it with baking parchment. Spoon the mixture in four tall piles, stroking the mixture with the back of the spoon to form smooth shiny peaks. Stud them with fresh cranberries and thin strips of glossy orange rind and bake for 1¼ hours.

3 Carefully turn over the meringues. If they do not peel away from the paper easily, put them back in the oven for 15 to 20 minutes and try again. Bake the upturned meringues for a further 20 minutes.

pistachio meringues

Pistachios add a wonderful nutty flavour to these delicate meringues which look pretty with summer fruits. Paired with vanilla ice cream they also make a perfect tea-time treat served with a cup of fragrant Earl Grey or a delicate summery tisane.

MAKES 10

FOR THE MERINGUE
150 g/5 oz/²/₃ cup large egg whites
300 g/11 oz/1¹/₂ cups caster (superfine) sugar
40 g/1¹/₂ oz/scant ¹/₂ cup pistachio nuts, finely chopped

FOR THE FILLING
One quantity of Vanilla cream (see page 9)

TO SERVE
15 g/¹/₂ oz/scant ¹/₄ cup pistachio nuts, crushed
450 g/1 lb/2 cups ripe strawberries

1 Preheat the oven to 150°C (300°F). Whisk the egg whites with the sugar in a bowl over a pan of simmering water, making sure the bottom of the bowl does not touch the water. Whisk until the egg white mixture is thick enough to form a trail when the whisk is removed.

2 Remove the bowl from the pan and continue to whisk until the mixture has cooled and is thick and shiny. Lightly fold in the nuts and spoon the mixture into 2¹/₂-cm (1-in) round piles onto baking trays lined with baking parchment. Bake for 1 to 1¹/₄ hours until the meringues easily peel away from the paper. Turn them over and leave to cook in the oven for a further 15 minutes until they are evenly textured and crisp throughout.

3 Pair the meringues with the vanilla cream. Sprinkle with extra crushed pistachio nuts and serve with fresh strawberries.

CREDITS

All the sugars in this book were supplied by Whitworths sugars (www.whitworths-sugar.com)

All the cakes in this book were prepared with The Kitchen Machine/Cake Mixer from the Kitchen Hardware Professional Range by Morphy Richards (www.morphy richards.co.uk)

For loaning china, glassware and bakeware, thanks go to Divertimenti (www.divertimenti.co.uk)

I would also like to thank Camilla Schneideman from the Divertimenti Café for the Victoria sponge recipe page 45.

For the fondant recipe page 10, I would like to thank the Cordon Bleu Culinary Art School (www.cordonbleu.net)

With thanks for the blue biscuit jar and measuring spoons, from Nigella Lawson's Living Kitchen Collection from Bliss (Tel: 44 (0)1789 400077)

For the muffin tins and various baking tins, Alan Silverwood Ltd (Tel: 44 (0)121 454 3571)

Tunisian recipes inspired by the Tunisian National Tourist Office (www.cometotunisia.co.uk)